OTHER VOICES, OTHER TIMES...

Hungry Hill Remembered

JOAN MORRIS REILLY

Also by Joan Morris Reilly
A Hungry Hill Trinity

ISBN: 147004577X
ISBN 13: 9781470045777

OTHER VOICES, OTHER TIMES...

Hungry Hill Remembered

JOAN MORRIS REILLY

For all whose roots and hearts will forever live on Hungry Hill

ACKNOWLEDGEMENTS

Many years ago, Dan Sullivan and Frank Faulkner published a popular monthly magazine called *"Hungry Hill"* to which I contributed stories frequently. The magazine has been out of business for several years but the interest and genuine fondness for the neighborhood remains and the old issues are valuable sources of reference. This book is a sequel to my first collection of memories, *"A Hungry Hill Trinity"* self-published in 2010, which told of three generations in my family who spent the better part of their lives on Hungry Hill. The favorable response to that book inspired me to record the stories of other people who lived there.

Though the neighborhood was synonymous with the Irish, there were several other ethnic groups who shared our lives and our time. For this book, I concentrated on the larger communities of Italians and Greeks as well as the small Jewish enclave that lived and worked on Hungry Hill.

I am extremely grateful to retired Judge Dan Keyes and Murray Harris for their part in this book. Their contributions and outstanding recall made them invaluable resources. I enjoyed the many interviews and correspondence with John

Serra and his sister Louise Laroche, Miceál Carney, Louise Speliopoulos, *Republican* columnist Tommy Shea, retired Judge Ann (Martin) Gibbons, Sister Kathleen Keating, Jane Doherty O'Donoghue, Jim (Red) Garvey, Bobby (Bo) Fitzgerald, Tom (Gomo) and Bob Welch, Jim Harrigan, Faith Karamallis Perrault, Manny Rovithis, Theresa Conway Balboni, Tom Shea's daughter, Mary, the Tougias brothers and many others who gave me their time and their thoughts.

The cooperation of Joe Christofori and his Hungry Hill Website and the use of his logo and photos was most appreciated as was the cover photo taken by Beth Reilly and the photo processing by Chris Murphy.

I was lucky to have the ongoing support of my children, Jim and Beth, and all that they contribute with their editing and photographic talents. Kudos to my sister Cheryl who took my cover idea and made it come to life and my niece, Amy Perrault, who gave it a professional finish.

As always, sincere thanks for the resources and the staff at the archives of the Springfield Museum of History. They are truly assets to our community.

Joan Morris Reilly

FOREWORD

I was born in 1918 in a two-tenement house at the corner of Liberty and Phoenix streets in a section of Springfield, Massachusetts called Hungry Hill. During the first part of the twentieth century, Hungry Hill could best be described as a small, tightly-knit neighborhood, populated by a friendly, gregarious people, bonded by a heritage of suffering and desolation; a people who could be brawling, quarrelsome, and at times hostile, but who, even in their worst moments, were men and women with virtues and human failings circumscribed by an unwavering faith in their Catholicism, and in a loving God's infinite mercy and justice.

They were hard working, intensely loyal, deeply religious and family oriented. Mercurial in temperament, inordinately opinionated, they were quick to reach out with compassion to those less fortunate, yet as previously noted, could be at times, resentful and intolerant toward those embracing different religious and political beliefs. Indeed, some of this was even directed toward their fellow Irish who resided in the plushy bedroom community of Longmeadow, or in the Forest Park and East Forest Park sections of Springfield, and thereby, presumably, enjoyed a superior social rank. These were referred to by the Hungry Hillers as "the lace curtain Irish," the "cut-glass Irish," or the "tt" (two toilet) Irish.

Looking back on the first chapter of my life, I remember above all, the accumulated character and experience of a great people, united by that inner strength and sense of purpose which has enabled people in every age to persevere and endure in the face of adversity.

What a great people they were! What a great place to be born and spend the formative years of my life! Mine has been credited in some quarters as being "The Greatest Generation." Were we? I don't know, but what I do know is that I would not want to have lived my 92 years (and any time I have left) at any other period in the history of mankind, or in any other place on earth.

Daniel M. Keyes, Jr.

TABLE OF CONTENTS

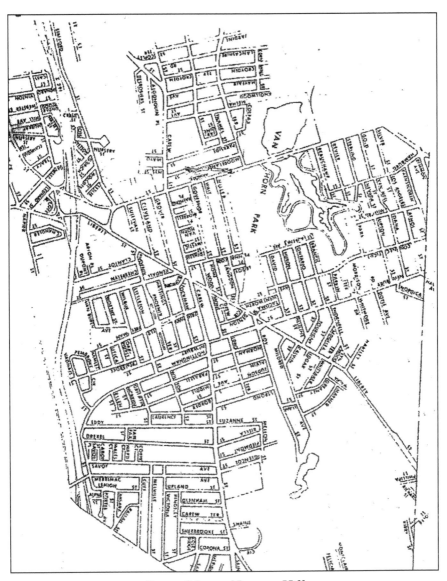

Street Map – Hungry Hill
City of Springfield, MA – 1988

HUNGRY HILL
LANDSCAPE

THE MAKING OF A NEIGHBORHOOD

According to the City Planning Department, Hungry Hill covers the areas bounded by Narragansett Street, the main east-west railroad tracks and Interstate 291, St. James Avenue and the Chicopee city line. Carew Street, a main artery, runs from Main Street in the North End through East Springfield to Chicopee. At one time, it was called Morgan Road east from Prospect Street.

The Hungry Hill neighborhood developed later than others in Springfield. In the 1880s, there were only a few scattered houses on the hill. Between 1868 and 1914, the area of Phoenix Terrace and other streets south of Liberty and Carew was the site of the Adventist Camp Meeting, (still called the campgrounds). The Camp Meeting drew thousands of Adventists from around the country for prayer and teaching. Attendees stayed in tents and eventually built small, one-and-a-half story cottages. When the campgrounds closed and the area developed as residential streets, some of the cottages were moved and used as homes. My grandfather and his brother each bought one of the campground houses. I was told that the price was one dollar with the understanding that you had to move it.

Both of these houses have had additions over the years and still stand on Laurence Street.

The first streets to be built up were Liberty, Armory, Stafford, Grover and Cleveland. The basic Hungry Hill house is the two-family. Between 1900 and 1930, rows of two-family houses went up on Mooreland, Parkside, Governor, Miller, Hastings and Clantoy Streets. Most units have six rooms and double porches. The two-family dwellings allowed one family to rent out another floor, a popular way for the owner to pay the mortgage and the renter to enjoy decent accommodations. The three-family houses came in two types, those built by adding a floor to the standard two-family house and the long narrow buildings with flat roofs, which are more prevalent in Worcester and Boston than in Springfield. Many immigrants made the two and three deckers of Hungry Hill their first home in America.

Dan Keyes recalls that a notable exception to the two and three family houses was the "Bee Hive," a large sprawling-like three-story habitation that strung along Liberty Street between Grover and Cleveland, with accommodations for 8 or 10 families. The Bee Hive was off-limits to him and his siblings due to the widely held belief that the dilapidated, slum-like, unsanitary condition of the premises made it a source of sickness and disease. By 1917, bungalows were built on Phoenix and Freeman Terraces and single-family colonials were built on Chapin Terrace and Melha Avenue.

After World War II, many of the streets between Newbury and St. James Avenue filled out with single-family ranches and capes and many from the older part of the Hill moved here and on to East Springfield.

The old Hungry Hill neighborhood was actually divided into separate enclaves. Each area was defined by small business enterprises, e.g. drug stores, markets and athletic teams.

Van Horn, the area between Van Horn Park and Our Lady of Hope at Armory and Carew and extending south on Armory to Stafford Street, had Millanes Drug Store and Leo's Van Horn Spa and of course Van Horn Park with its numerous athletic teams

Blackstones – the team name for the area around Sampson Funeral Home, along Phoenix Street to Kendall Street. Kazin's Drug Store was located in this stretch.

Americans – Team name of the area covering Wilbur Street, Freeman Terrace and Newbury St. to Carey's farm on Hamlet Street. Vezina's Drug Store was their landmark.

Bluebirds –Team name for Newbury Street to Liberty and Newbury to East Springfield the other way. The Carew Pharmacy (Dave's Drug Store) was the center of this area.

TRANSPORTATION

In the early days, the principal and for a long time the only methods of transportation were by foot and by trolley car. Automobile ownership was almost unheard of on the Hill and it was not unusual to walk from one end of the city to the other to watch a ballgame or attend some social event. School transportation was nonexistent, and according to Dan Keyes, he walked back and forth to school—sometimes as much as two miles each way, in all kinds of weather.

The trolley car was a conveyance made to accommodate 25 to 30 passengers and ran on parallel metal tracks laid along the center of the city's main arteries. It collected electric current from an overhead cable strung above the tracks, which was transmitted to the car's motor by a wire suspended from the cable. Both Liberty and Carew Streets had trolley routes. The fare was five cents (increased later on to ten) and if a passenger wished to travel further or in a different direction than the original route, he or she would be given a transfer ticket for use on another trolley which would take them to their destination.

In addition to the trolley cars on Liberty Street, there was a small bus-like vehicle called a jitney, which carried passengers between the Hungry Hill section and the downtown area at a cost of five cents a passenger. The operator during the summer months was a young, Holy Cross College student by the name of James F. Egan, who later on became one of Springfield's most prominent attorneys.

The Springfield Street Railway was the first bus system in Springfield and bus routes ran through Hungry Hill from downtown – Carew to East Springfield line and the Falls by Liberty run.

Early Social life and Entertainment

One of the most popular forms of relaxation for the adult population on Hungry Hill in the decades of the twenties and thirties was the "kitchen racket." A "kitchen racket" was an open-invitation event usually held in someone's home on Saturday night. Dan Keyes remembers that the purpose of these get-togethers was to spend an evening of sociability and good fellowship, leavened by the imbibitions of a bit of the poteen. An attendee was expected to donate fifty cents or a dollar for the privilege of participating in the festivities and invariably, there was standing room only. Usually the women gathered in the living room or front part of the house, while the men congregated in the kitchen and out in the back yard. Along about midnight, what had started as a quiet, pleasant, companionable gathering of the clan often developed into a boisterous, raucous disputatious brouhaha!

Listening to the radio in the 1930s was an everyday event and many on Hungry Hill, like 30 million other Americans, listened faithfully to Father Charles Coughlin. Father Coughlin was an Irish Catholic priest who was credited with being one of the major demagogues of the 20th century and was able to influence politics

through broadcasting without actually holding a political office himself. He was a strong
believer in the need for social reform and supported Franklin Roosevelt and the New Deal
but later became a harsh critic of Roosevelt and
turned against him spouting conspiracy and anti-
Semitism theories. Father Coughlin defended
the activities of the Nazi government and even
Theodore Geisel, (Dr. Seuss) attacked him in the
press, calling him a Nazi sympathizer.

Agnes Reavey of Springfield once ran for
governor and was considered a "Father Coughlin candidate" as he openly supported her.

Coughlin was the frontrunner of radio personalities of today like Rush Limbaugh and Glenn
Beck; loud public figures who capitalize on fear
during a poor economy. Their rhetoric is laced
with scapegoating, ridicule and paranoia and
like Father Coughlin, they often talk of conspiracy and anti-semitism. The difference between
today's "shock jocks" and Father Coughlin is
today they have different targets for their hatred
and are more powerful than Coughlin. The radio
audience of the 1930s looked to the radio for
local and national news, music, drama and religious offerings, which were just as important to
them as Father Coughlin's opinions.

HUNGRY HILL LANDMARKS

Like so many local landmarks all over America there are many that identify with the Hungry Hill community.

Springfield Boys Club has a long history in Springfield dating back to 1891. It stood on the corner of Chestnut and Ferry Streets until 1967 when it was demolished for the North End Urban Renewal Project. That year, the Boys Club moved up to Carew Street to the property known as the blackberry patch or Hendee Park.

Shriners Hospital for Crippled Children. In 1922, the Shriners chose Springfield over Boston to establish a hospital for crippled children in New England. The Shriners do not charge children's families or third-party insurers. The original hospital was designed by Max Westoff with Ionic columns. This building was replaced with a larger, more modern hospital.

Gurdon Bill Park at the corner of Liberty and Genesee Streets is the former site of the Gurdon Bill Estate called "Vineland." The house is long gone but the wooded ravines have been a city park since 1920. Gurdon Bill was one of Springfield's business leaders in the latter 19th century. He was a publisher, president of the Springfield & New London Railroad and President of the

Second National Bank of Springfield. He served on the City Council and in the Massachusetts House of Representatives.

Armory Street Fire Station The architect was B.H. Seabury who designed many of the city's other fire stations. The fire station's tower was used to hang and dry the hoses.

Van Horn Park between Miller Street and Chapin Terrace on the south and Beauchamp and Cunningham Streets on the north—this 120-acre park originally was Springfield's water supply reservoir. Its use as a reservoir was discontinued in 1908 and it was turned into a city park. On the corner of Miller Street and Armory, the Hampden County Truant School stood from 1872 to 1916. After it closed, the farmland that the Truant School had used was turned into athletic fields. In 1922, a wooden grandstand seating 1200 was erected at the main baseball diamond, the scene of countless youth, high school and semi-pro games. The grandstand was replaced by bleachers in 1953. Two years later the Van Horn Field House and the John L. Sullivan monument were dedicated. John L. Sullivan had been the "The King of the Kids," the founder of little league baseball in Springfield. To this day, Van Horn Park offers many ball fields, basketball and tennis courts, a playground, excellent trails for walking, jogging, or biking, and acres of woodland.

St. Benedict's cemetery on the south side of Liberty Street at the I-291 rotary, was named for the first Catholic church in Springfield, which was located near Union and Willow Streets. All its plots were sold by 1884, when St. Michael's took over as the preeminent Catholic cemetery in Springfield.

Liberty Café on Liberty Street has the distinction of being issued the first license to serve alcohol after Prohibition was repealed in 1933.

American Legion Post 430 The original building was opened in 1953. In 1978, the A&P replaced the original building with a supermarket and the Post built new quarters behind the A&P.

T.P. Sampson Funeral Home Any social history of the Hill should include Sampson's, which has been the scene of thousands of neighborhood wakes. It was opened in 1930 as the John B. Shea Colonial Funeral Parlor. Prior to this, wakes on Hungry Hill took place in the houses of the deceased. Neylon Sampson started the Sampson family tradition, followed by T.P. Sampson and currently, John Sampson.

The Liberty Branch Library was originally located in the basement of the Liberty Methodist

Church. It moved into its own building designed by architect Max Westoff in 1931. This and other branch libraries were paid for with private funds by a bequest from Andrew Carnegie and other donors.

Liberty Methodist Church The "other" church on Hungry Hill, started as a mission and met in a house at Cleveland and Liberty Streets in 1900. Five years later, the mission built a church on the east corner of Liberty and Carew Streets. The congregation dedicated the present gothic structure on January 1, 1922.. This church took an active role in the Hungry Hill Community. As mentioned above, the basement of the church was the original Liberty Branch Library. Many Boy Scout and Girl Scout meetings were held there and, it was an active election precinct.

Bottle Park is a triangle at the intersection of Carew and Liberty Streets. This has long been considered the geographic heart of Hungry Hill. The name was changed to Brunton Park in 1984 and dedicated to former Mayor Daniel B. Brunton, a Hungry Hill resident.

Tougias Bakery is a fixture on Hungry Hill since 1947 located at Liberty and Woodmont Streets, formerly called The Athens Bakery. This bakery has been in the same family for three generations beginning with Elias Tougias, who immigrated from Greece in the 1890s. The current owners, Steve and David, make the bread the same way their grandfather did, using all natural ingredients, no chemicals or additives.

Abbe Farm at 998 Liberty Street belonged to one of Springfield's most prominent families and it stretched to the Chicopee line. The Gothic Revival house has gables with gingerbread decoration.

Hogan's Ice & Fuel at 1173 Liberty Street. is the oldest house in this part of the city and was, for a long time, a farmhouse for the Searle family. Since 1926 it belonged to the Hogan family. The land attached to the house includes the Abbe Brook area (which once was Chicopee's water supply), a pond used for ice cutting. In the 1950s the area was developed for residential streets like Whittaker, Greaney and Mayher Streets.

WGGB-TV Channel 40 This ABC affiliate grew out of WHYN Radio, which originated in Holyoke in 1941. The television station was established in 1953 as Channel 55 on Mt. Tom. where its transmitter still stands. A year later, the station moved its studios to more spacious quarters on Liberty Street, one of the highest points in Springfield. This site enabled Channel

55 to transmit its signal to the Mt. Tom transmitter.

Springfield Shopping Plaza This land was originally owned by farmer John Abbe, the first settler in this area. It was an athletic park before becoming the Springfield Airport in 1927. The sirport was home of the Gee Bee airplanes built by the Granville family. In 1931, Lowell Bayles set the world air speed record in a Gee Bee. Maude Tait, who also flew out of the Springfield Airport, set the speed record for women that year. In 1953, developers announced plans to build a shopping center with 7500 parking spaces at the vast airfield. Six years later the Springfield Plaza opened with 4000 parking spaces, hundreds of which have never been used. It remains one of the largest strip malls in Western Mass.

Marconi Club Built by the Italian population on Hungry Hill more than 70 years ago, the Marconi Club is located on a corner that encompasses Parallel Street, Wilson and Middle Streets. In its heyday, it was a popular spot for weddings as well as for ongoing bocce tournaments.

OUR LADY OF HOPE CHURCH

The Beginning

Our Lady of Hope Church was built on the crest of Hungry Hill at 743 Armory Street and is one of Springfield's most prominent landmarks. The parish was started in 1906 to serve the 600 or so Catholics living in Hungry Hill and East Springfield. A simple wooden church on the east side of Armory Street sufficed until the 1920s when the parishioners built a grand Italian renaissance edifice. Pastor James Cruse said the first Mass in the church basement in 1926 and twelve years later the church was completed. By this time, the parish had grown to 7700 members.

Our Lady of Hope was designed by diocesan architect John W. Donohue and is modeled after Santo Spirito in Florence, Italy. Our Lady of Hope's relationship to the neighborhood was almost European. The bell tower is visible from many points in the area and for many years, you could hear the bells signaling Mass, the Angelus, Noon and Matins.

For many years, there were four priests assigned to the church and there were numerous Sunday Masses scheduled every hour from 7:00 a.m. to 11 a.m. For those attending the later

Masses, there was a choice of going to mass in the upstairs church or in the basement church. Both were usually filled to capacity.

For at least half a century, Our Lady of Hope was Hungry Hill's central social institution and much of the Hill's community life centered around church activities. There were Monday night novenas; vesper service; the bi-annual minstrel shows which featured local talent like Bob Fisk and later, Bruce Fitzgerald; Drum Corps; baseball teams; the Ladies Sodality and the men's monthly Holy Name meetings with their annual retreat at the Monastery in West Springfield. In later years, when the lower church was closed, the Hope Center moved into the basement and served as a senior center, a social center, and headquarters for the Hungry Hill Neighborhood Council.

During the 1940s, 1950s and 1960s, high numbers were the norm at Our Lady of Hope. First Communion and Confirmation classes were exceptionally large. There was hardly a Saturday that several weddings didn't take place.

But, change is the only certainty in life and, this does not exclude churches. The Catholic Church made many liturgical changes in the last few decades. For example, Mass is now said in English not Latin and the priest faces the congregation instead of the altar. There is more participation by those attending Mass and there is a choice of taking communion in your hand or having the priest or extraordinary minister place it in your mouth. Another change is the elimination of paying fifteen cents at the door. I can close my eyes and still see the late Danny Brunton, then the mayor of Springfield, sitting in the foyer of the church making change and collecting the fee. Maggie Gilhooley played the organ for the men's choir and prayers for the recently departed always included someone who died in Ireland.

Physical changes at Our Lady of Hope included the removal of the baldacchino (canopy) around the altar and the very long communion rail. Through these aesthetic changes, the church remained solidly intact and true to the words engraved over the entrance – "In loco isto dabo pacem" (in this place I shall give peace). In addition to peace, one had a sense of belonging—a rare thing and something to cherish in a world that grows progressively colder.

The End

A major restructuring of the Springfield Diocese resulted in numerous school and church closings. In 2009, the diocese released a list of churches that were to be closed and it included Our Lady of Hope. The news of the closing was met with disbelief and sorrow by current and former parishioners. This church had played an enormous part in the lives of so many families, who, like myself, could never imagine that it would not always be there. I borrow from Mark Twain whose words seem to echo the sentiments of so many people affected by the closing ... *"It was of us and we were in its confidence and lived in its grace and in the peace of its benediction.....we could not enter it unmoved."*

At the closing mass, which was held on New Year's eve 2009, at 4:00 p.m., there was a line of cars on Carew Street, beginning at Liberty, waiting to make a left-hand turn onto Armory Street. It was standing room only–people stood along the walls on both sides of the church.

The Mass was beautifully done, complete with a bagpiper and several priests who were native sons of Hungry Hill. Msgr. Joyce was gracious and reassuring and reminded everyone that he was just a phone call away. The choir was outstanding and everyone joined in on *"Auld Lang*

Syne" and the "*Irish Blessing*" at the end of the service, which left many of us teary-eyed.

The final chapter of this 103 year-old story was presented with dignity and pride and truly marked the end of an era.

AMERICAN LEGION POST 430

Some gave all...all gave some

Like every neighborhood in America, Hungry Hill lost young men in World War II—The ones I know of are John Rossini, Frank Hogan and Joe O'Brien from Liberty Street, Dominic Vechiarelli from Grover Street and John Cabey of Laurence Street who died at St. Lowe in France. The Cormier family of Littleton Street lost two sons and Nottingham Street lost William Sullivan, who was killed in the Battle of the Bulge and Edmund Wynne in the Pacific, who was taken prisoner when his ship was torpedoed. Others included Howard Welch, Raymond Shea, Patrick O'Donnell, Alexander Sawicki, Jackie Donlin, Jackie Mack, Billy Maloney, Joe Fenton, Les Lehr, Henry Mastrianni, Luke Dean, Bill Sullivan of Stockman Street, Harold Macney and John Haggerty.

Some of them are memorialized in this area. There's a street in Springfield known as Edmund Wynne Circle which is located in a housing project built after World War II. Also, Luke Dean's name is on a chalice at St. Mary's Church and John Cabey is remembered by a stained glass window at this same church, (now Mary, Mother of Hope Church).

American Legion Liberty Post 430 was started by 23 World War II vets who had grown up in the Liberty Heights section of Springfield. A temporary charter was issued in 1948 with 14 charter members: Thomas E. O'Connell, John J. Fitzgerald, John P. Beasley, James J. Murphy, John R. Davin, James F. Woods, Patrick M. Courtney, William J. Foley, Sylvester F. Burke, John A. Opitz, William D. Garvey, Francis J. Rice, Harry F. Tighe and Maurice J. Hoar.

The Marconi Club became the unofficial post home until 1949 when they acquired six and one-half acres of land on Liberty Street from the Water Department.

A bond drive was initiated to build new headquarters. Congressman Eddie Boland served as chairman and he also headed the Building Committee after $40,000 was raised. This undertaking was a "Do it Ourselves" project relying heavily on the membership which consisted of various tradesmen and skilled workers who gave generously of their help and labor as well as scores of other individuals and firms in the city. The community building of Liberty Heights Post 430 was opened on April 25, 1953. The dedication took place in October 1953 with Senator John F. Kennedy giving the address.

When the new building was dedicated in 1953, the membership total was close to 600. With the exception of Maurice Kantor, many past commanders were of Irish descent: Beasley, Rice, McKenna, O'Connor, Hogan snd, Conway but, the membership was an ethnic stew. The roster included many Irish names like Ashe, Begley, Boland, Cabey, Carey, Dillon, Fitzgerald, Garvey, Haggerty, Kennedy, Long, Lynch, Maloney, Murphy, O'Brien, O'Connell, Ryan, Sullivan, Sweeney, Walsh and Wynne but there was just as many non-Irish names like Beaulieu, Bono, Busansky, Choquette, Christofori, DeBonis, Fantoni, Gobeille, Gatti, Guynup, Iuliano, Kantor, Karam, Klenyklaus, Kreuger, Lacedonia, Lamoureux, Megazzini, Papageorge, Pasini, Pouliot, Salerno, Stahovich, Serra, Turcotte, Tyburski, Vecchiarelli, Wroblewski, Zimmerman, Zeo, Zuffelato and many more. The Liberty Post veterans were truly a multicultural group all with the same dream – to have their own legion post/community center in their own neighborhood.

The Women's Auxiliary was founded in 1950. The wives, mothers, daughters and sisters of any member of the American Legion were invited to join and assist in the bond drive for the common goal of a new headquarters building. Once the new building was a reality, they got involved in child welfare programs for needy veterans and destitute families, rehabilitation and various community drives. They equipped and outfitted the Post 430 10-12 sandlot baseball team and they made it possible for girls to attend Girls State, a department program to educate girls in the role of government. Another function of the auxiliary was recalled by longtime member, Theresa Conway Balboni, who spoke of the many hours spent cooking and preparing food for the numerous Post 430 events.

The auxiliary charter members were: Mary Hogan Allen, Anita Bousquet, Josephine Barrett, Florence Christofori, Mary Connor, Loretta Coughlin, Verna Cunningham, Lillian Curley, Eleanor Curran, Mary A. Daly, Margaret DeMaria, Eileen Fahey, Mary Fahey, Mary Fenton, Margaret Fitzgerald, Marguerite Foley, Columbine Fontaine, Bridget Garvey, Catherine Gra, Rose Harrigan, Pearl Harte, Rita Harte, Rita M. Harte, Rosalie Hickey, Kathleen Hoar, Anna Hogan, Mary Hogan, Isabel Kane, Margaret Kreuger, Mary Leonard, Mary Lyons, Kathryn Linnehan, Mary Linnehan, Alice Mitchell, Annette Mitchell, Helen Morin, Elizabeth Morris, Marion Morris, Mary Muske,; Enis Nelson, Mary J. O'Connor, Daisy O'Connor, Lena Piacentini, Dorothy Regan, Marion Sheremeta,

Ann Sullivan, Mary Sullivan, Edna Tourangeau, Helen Vadnais, Marie Vezina and Mary Walsh.

Sadly, as buildings go, Post 430 had a short life span. Some 25 years later the original building, the dream realized by so many Liberty Heights people, disappeared into memory, replaced by a new building which was eventually sold due to declining membership. Currently, the membership stands at about 100 and is a very diverse group. At this writing, the Commander was Dan Hamre and they held meetings in downtown Springfield at the GAR Building.

The late Bibbers Dalton wrote about the Post 430 members in his "Springfield Original Nine" poem: ....*"they were looking for more marchers for that grand St. Patrick's Day and could Hungry Hill's Irish help in any way? Well they put their heads together, "Willum" Garvey and Tom Shea; Midge Reilly and Gene Leonard were going all the way. Frank Carey and Tom Landers gave approval too, Franny Rice with Tom Foley thought the plan would do. Dante Christofori, Hungry Hill's Italian son, agreed with Tommy Landers, all would have great fun. Post 430 caught the spirit and was ready to the man, Hungry Hill had given its pledge, they were there when it began........"*

HOGAN'S ICE COMPANY/LIBERTY ICE & FUEL

By Murray Harris

It was probably around 1930 when I first met Mr. Peter Hogan.

My parents operated Harris Market on Liberty Street, at the corner of Grover Street. In those early days, refrigeration had not been developed and food had to be preserved with ice which was supplied by Hogan's. In our market, we had a walk-in icebox and meat case that required the delivery of many 100 pound cakes of ice.

My father had a small green Ford truck for delivering groceries that was also used to bring ice twice weekly to our store. The access door on the icebox was about 4 feet above ground and it required great strength to lift the 100-pound cakes of ice to install them in the compartment.

Many times when my father went to pick up the ice, I would accompany him. I was very young when I first saw Mr. Hogan. He lived at that time on Woodmont Street and behind his house, there was a large building for storing the 100-pound cakes of ice. Peter Hogan was a serious, rugged-looking individual who was all business. He was very impressive to watch as he worked on the front platform, wearing hip boots folded down and wielding a pair of ice tongs to handle the cakes of ice.

Later he moved his company to upper Liberty Street adjacent to the Springfield Airport. There were two ponds on that property that produced ice in the wintertime. Mr. Hogan, his sons, and a crew harvested the ice from the larger pond which they stored in two huge barns nearby.

Hogan's ice trucks plied the streets of Hungry Hill. The drivers kept a keen eye on house windows to spot the "ice cards." The cards had markings on all four sides to designate how much ice they wanted. As kids, we would gather around the trucks and when the driver would use an ice pick to quarter the cakes of ice, we would grab up the ice shavings. It was a treat for us especially on warm summer days.

Mr. Hogan made a vital contribution to the necessities of life at that time. He kept the ice-boxes in the homes and businesses filled with fresh cakes of ice to preserve perishable foods. When electrical refrigeration became available, the demand for ice lessened, but Mr. Hogan's ingenuity and the Hogan Ice Company will never be forgotten by those who lived on Hungry Hill during that period.

HUNGRY HILL SCHOOLS

Armory Street School - the first public school on Hungry Hill was a one-room wooden structure erected in 1885 to serve the families clustered around Armory, Liberty and Stafford Streets. The brick building was built in 1902 and the rear wing was added seven years later. The school was demolished in the 1970s and a new modern elementary school was built named for Congressman Edward Boland.

Our Lady of Hope School – 625 Carew Street, was designed in 1920 by John Donohue. This building became the Christian Education Center in 1964 when a new school was built by Father John Power on Armory Street, adjacent to the church. The original building was demolished and a Walgreen's Drug Store now stands in that spot. The school was closed by the Diocese and is now owned by the City of Springfield and operates as Zanetti School.

Liberty School – 962 Carew Street, was built in 1918 during World War I when the U.S. government sold Liberty bonds and sauerkraut was called Liberty cabbage. Presumably, this influenced the city fathers in the naming of Liberty School. Principals in the early years included Miss Wilson and then Miss Sheehan.

Glenwood School - Morison Terrace was originally named by George Atwater to describe the character of the area which lies between Van Horn Park and Chicopee. The first school was located on the Springfield, Armory and Silver Street Triangle. When the new school on Morison Terrace was completed in 1930, it was considered the "most up-to-date of the city schools." Bricks from the old school were used to build two houses on Silver Street facing the triangle, one on Springfield Street and two on Caseland Street. Principals included Margaret Davison and Marguerite Sheehan, who was once the principal of Liberty School.

Van Sickle Junior High School - 1170 Carew Street, was built in 1931 and named for Springfield School Superintendent James Hixon Van Sickle. Van Sickle was the city's first school to be built specifically as a junior high. It incorporated the latest in vocational and home economics training. It was built midway between Hungry Hill and East Springfield to serve both neighborhoods. The school was modernized in the 1970s and a swimming pool was added.

LOMBARD RESERVOIR A/K/A HALLWRIGHTS (HORIZE)

Hungry Hill's field of dreams

A popular place for decades of Hungry Hill kids was Hallwrights or Horize depending on which decade you were there. This consisted of a reservoir in a wooded area at the end of Freeman Terrace near the railroad tracks with sand hills and open spaces. It was a great place to go sledding and ice skating in the winter and the sandy area of the reservoir served as a "BAB" in the summer. Also, the reservoir was a good place to catch frogs and polliwogs.

The Lombard Reservoir was officially closed down in 1920 by the City of Springfield. Beyond the reservoir was the Howes Sand Company, on the edge of the tracks. After it was closed down by the city, it became a dumping ground. During the Depression years, junk cars and trucks were dumped there. During World War II, one man brought a power shovel there to take out the junk cars so they could be melted down for the war effort. After the war, the Springfield Armory used the area to dump trash. Also, the nearby Cheney Bigelow Wire Works would dump ashes there.

This area became Freeman Park when the residents appealed to State Representative Hooper Walsh, to have a park located there. Msgr. Farland and Beverly Ruggeri kept the park in good condition. Alfred and Aggie Mandrellas, whose house was adjacent to the park, spent 30 years scheduling games there and keeping the area clean. Eventually, the park deteriorated from sinkholes caused from all the dumping that went on in the past. In addition, a bad element was frequenting the park involving drug activity. so the police shut the park down.

Since then, part of the reservoir was taken, including the chimney drain, for Interstate Route 291. Recent activities indicate that it might be making the full circle as truckloads of dirt have been brought into the area and grass has been planted. There is talk of it becoming a park again.

Courtesy of Chris Murphy Photography

Lombard Reservoir a/k/a Hallwrights/Horize

HUNGRY HILL'S ANIMAL KINGDOM

Two-headed goats, some long-neck geese and other notable species

When Hungry Hill was first settled and well into the 1950s, besides the usual cat and dogs for pets, many barnyard animals, cows, goats, horses, geese, chickens and ducks could be found, mostly in the Liberty Heights section of Hungry Hill which was more countrified with woods, dirt roads, and a lot of undeveloped land.

Some of the animal stories are material for "Ripley's Believe it or Not." The Careys on Hamlet Street raised pigs and a cow, which rumor has it, was accidently shot one night by a policeman who was walking the beat at night and in the darkness, thought the cow was a bear or some other wild animal. Mr. Carey also had a horse named "Old Dan." This horse was invaluable for projects like helping the Cabeys move their campground houses to Laurence Street. The Serra Family of Hamlet Street raised chickens and rabbits. At one time they had as many as 30 rabbits during World War II. Wartime resulted in many shortages but the Serras were never without meat to feed their large family, thanks to the chickens and the rabbits.

Numerous families raised goats. The Sherwoods and the Guynups of Border Street had goats as did the Daras Family of Griffin Street. This was very beneficial to families with babies who could not tolerate cow's milk. Their milk was used to make cheese also. Patricia Cabey Reardon recalls visiting Mrs. Daras with her grandmother. Mrs. Daras was a Greek lady, an herbalist, who would gather leaves and roots to make teas to cure various ailments. She also shared homeopathic remedies. During one of my few visits to Mrs. Daras with my great-aunt and my cousin, I remember her telling Auntie Mary that the secret to staying young was to walk barefoot through grass that had morning dew on it!

The Daras family had numerous goats and at some point in the 1940s had a two-headed baby goat! This was a very rare phenomenon and it wasn't expected to live very long. When Patricia saw it, she loved it and wanted to keep it as a pet.

Chickens were everywhere at that end of Hungry Hill. Growing up on Laurence Street consisted of more than one rooster crowing every morning. Patricia Reardon also recalled that one family in the area had chickens who wore eyeglasses! This was done to prevent the chickens from pecking each other. They are aggressive barnyard animals and when blood was drawn on the chicken at the bottom of the pecking order, the others would go into a frenzy and peck it to death. Farm catalogs used to offer the glasses for sale. They had aluminum frames with red plastic lenses about the size of dimes and were fastened to the chicken's beak with a cotter pin. The rose-colored glasses made everything look the same color and made them virtually colorblind. This improved their eating habits as well. Chicken feed used to contain red colored vitamins and the chickens would only eat the red seeds. So, with the glasses, the chickens ate all of their food and didn't fight with each other.

In many ways, chickens act a lot like humans. If one is being picked on, many will join in on the attack much like bullying in our world. Maybe society needs to have rose-colored glasses. Think of how peaceful life would be if we were all colorblind, ate the right food and got along with each other! In 1955, on the TV show, *What's My Line*, one contestant's occupation was making eyeglasses for chickens and he completely stumped the panel.

The Hogan Family of Liberty Street raised horses. On occasion, the horses would get loose and gallop around the neighboring streets. The Hogan family used to let Father Dave Sullivan, then a curate at Our Lady of Hope Church, ride their horses whenever he so desired. Also, Tom Pollard of Van Buren Street was a renowned horse trainer, a skill he learned in Ireland. There was once a stable to keep horses where St. Mary's Church is now located in East Springfield.

The Bill Cabey family of Laurence Street had their own menagerie of animals beginning with their dog Orphie, short for Orphan, who was basically the neighborhood dog. They also had a duck. Ducky Cabey sometimes visited Liberty School to swim in the courtyard fountain at the school. Then there was Friday, the gigantic goose who served as a "watchdog" for the premises. If anyone walked into the yard, Friday would spread his wings and run toward them hissing.

Fred "Tripoli" Alovis of Nottingham Street had several geese and they too fiercely guarded his property. Even the paper boy got chased away by the gaggle of geese. They also had a nanny goat, chickens and a dog.

As Liberty Heights became less of a country area and more of a city neighborhood, barnyard species gradually became inappropriate by virtue of ordinances, additional housing and less open space. The chickens, ducks, goats, geese, horses, cows and rabbits eventually disappeared. They can only be found now in smaller, more rural areas but once upon a time, they were part of everyday life on Hungry Hill.

Seeing Duck in the Drink Fun for Kids, Don't You Think?

Liberty School left to right, Susan, Buddy, Willie, Timmy and Ducky Cabey

The Cabey's had a friendly duck,
its down was white as snow

And everywhere the children went,
the duck would want to go,

It followed them to school one day
which was against the rule,

But how the students laughed and cheered
to see a duck in pool!

Springfield Daily News, May 26, 1955

HUNGRY HILL LEADERS
AND LEGENDS

HUNGRY HILL LEADERS AND LEGENDS

By Dan Keyes

I think of my old neighborhood – that once almost isolated enclave whose name origin is still shrouded in mystery, and I marvel at the extraordinary achievement and success of its first generation progeny. In my time, it has produced a Congressman, who served his district for 36 years – the District Attorney for the Western District of Massachusetts, three Mayors – the Sheriff of Hampden County – three Judges, three chiefs of police – a college president – the president of the largest savings bank in Western Massachusetts, dozens of priests and members of religious orders and countless men and women who achieved remarkable success in the business and professional life of the community. I venture that no other comparable community in America has contributed more to the common weal.

These "distinguished alums" of Hungry Hill include the following:

Edward Boland	U.S. Congressman, 36 yrs.
Matthew Ryan	District Atty. Hampden County, 32 years
John Curley	Sheriff, Hampden County
Daniel Brunton	Mayor, City of Springfield
Thomas O'Connor	Mayor, City of Springfield
William Sullivan	Mayor, City of Springfield
John Maloney	Chief of Police
John Lyons	Chief of Police
Paul Fenton	Chief of Police
Daniel M.Keyes	District Court Judge
Ann Martin Gibbons	District Court Judge
Eileen Griffin	Superior Court Judge
George Lawler	Chief, Spfld.Fire Dept.
Bill Jamer	CEO – Savings Bank
Charles Hough	Business Executive L.E. Belcher
Sr. Kathleen Keating	President, Elms College
Eleanor Powell	Renowned dancer, movie star

THE FIRST CAMPAIGN - MEMORIES OF EDDIE BOLAND

By Dan Keyes

Eddie Boland's journey from the obscure precincts of Hungry Hill to Beacon Hill to Capitol Hill is a story of American opportunity come true. One of my favorite memories is his first campaign and the emergence of the "Irish Mafia."

Nineteen thirty-four was a watershed year in the lives of Eddie Boland and myself. We had known each other for about three years and had become the closest of friends. He was the Daily News Sandlot Director and as such had endeared himself to the younger generation and many of their parents.

In that year, at the age of 23, he decided to run for representative to the Massachusetts Legislature from Springfield's Ward 2 (which then included Ward 8) against a three-term popular incumbent by the name of Ed "Doc" Cawley. Ward 2 included all of Hungry Hill and part of the lower Ward, all of which was predominantly Irish. It was a five-man race with it becoming apparent early on that Boland and Cawley were the main contenders. This election (actually a primary which was tantamount to election) saw the birth of the Irish Mafia, a contingent of Irish women, most of them from Dingle, County Kerry, and its environs, who campaigned door to door for Boland. They included Eddie's mother, my mother (Ma Keyes), Bridgie Johnson, Mary Keough, Mary Guiheen, Catherine Crohan, Helen Lynch, Mrs. Leahy, and a host of others who worked tirelessly, day after day for months for "Jo Boland's son, Edward." They held kitchen rackets, rallies in cellars, button-holed people on the street and in the market, campaigning with an almost missionary fervor for "one of our own."

On the Friday night before the primary, in an unprecedented demonstration, at least fifteen hundred kids, ages 10 to 21, from all over the city, marched up and down the streets of Hungry Hill in a torchlight parade for their friend Eddie Boland, winding up in a giant rally in the vacant lot next to the Armory Street fire station where Our Lady of Hope school now stands. Kids can't vote but they can influence their parents. I remember John Mack, who lived at the corner of Cleveland and Armory Streets right across from the school. He told me that he and his wife had always supported Doc Cawley; but when their son, 12-year old Jackie, threatened to run away from home if they didn't vote for Eddie Boland, they switched, and not only voted for Eddie but became two of his staunchest supporters.

In 1934, all the ballots were counted by hand. When the workers in each precinct finished counting, the precinct captain would call the election commissioner's office at the city or town hall and report the tally for that precinct. On primary night in 1934, we were at City Hall keeping tabs on the tally as the reports trickled in from Wards 2 and 8. Well past midnight, with all the ballots counted except those for Precinct D in Ward 2, Cawley's home precinct, Boland was leading by 30 votes. At last, shortly after 2 a.m., it was reported that Boland had carried Precinct D by 27 votes, giving him a victory total of 57. It should be pointed out that Precinct D was not only Cawley's bailiwick but the home turf of Bridgie Johnson and Mary Keough, two of the "mafia" stalwarts. They had delivered! It was the Irish Mafia's first campaign. It would not be their last.

As Eddie spread his political wings, they would go far afield into the cities and towns of the county and congressional district, enlisting the support of their compatriots and demonstrating a loyalty that was to be revisited time after time by themselves and their offspring over a period of fifty-four years. Their influence became universally recognized and for many years politicians throughout the area sought their help.

One last anecdote in connection with this campaign. When the news finally came in early that morning and Eddie's election was conceded, I had someone drive me to his Hungry Hill home on Mooreland Street where his mother and father were waiting for the results. I walked into the house and said to his mother, "Ma, Eddie won!" In true Irish fashion, she turned her eyes heavenward, clasped her hands together over her head and, "Glory be to God; we'll never see another poor day."

From time to time through the years, the news media would refer to the Boland-Keyes "organization." Truly, we never had any structured organization as such. What we did have were people; hundreds, even thousands of people from all over and their sons and daughters after them, who, throughout the 54 years of his public life, were unwavering in their loyalty and devotion to Eddie Boland.

REFLECTIONS ON DAN KEYES

By Murray Harris

I was born in 1917 and in 1921 entered into kindergarten at Armory Street School, located on Hungry Hill. Two of my fellow kindergarteners, Danny Keyes and Matty Ryan rose to prominence in political circles. Danny Keyes became a District Court Judge and Matty Ryan became District Attorney of Hampden County.

During our early years at school, I often played sports with Danny and Matty. Dan was an excellent athlete and excelled in baseball. Matty was a good athlete and a tough competitor. We played together in baseball and soccer and engaged in gymnastics at the school.

At various times in my life Dan was very helpful. Anytime I needed references, I went to him and his response was immediate. When I was 18 years old, I was in the naval service stationed in Chelsea, Massachusetts. Dan and I frequently rode the train together from Springfield and I often met him at South Station for the return trip to Springfield.

After Dan had passed the bar and entered into his law practice, he was recognized as a political strategist. When Governor Tobin was running for office, Dan became very heavily involved in the election campaign and his efforts helped the Governor to win. Later, Dan was made a District Court judge and at the time, was the youngest judge in the state.

I am proud to count him as one of my lifelong friends.

Remembering Matty Ryan

By Murray Harris

In 1921, my parents enrolled me in kindergarten at Armory Street School located on Hungry Hill in Springfield. At the same time, another pupil named Matthew J. Ryan, Jr. soon known as "Matty" became one of my classmates. As we progressed through the grades, we played sports together. Matty was a fine athlete and from day one a tough competitor.

He rose to political prominence when he became District Attorney of Western Massachusetts. When JFK began his candidacy for president in 1960, he chose Matty to be in charge of the state of New Jersey. Congressman Eddie Boland was placed in charge of Ohio. Both were tireless workers and producers for the Kennedy family.

The Kennedy headquarters for the state of New Jersey was located at the Hildebrand Hotel in Trenton. They occupied the entire mezzanine in the hotel. Matty had to make frequent trips to Trenton and it took five to six hours each way. He knew I had my own airplane so he hired me to fly him on round trips to Trenton.

One day, it was urgent for him to be in Trenton. A serious problem confronted JFK because Lyndon Johnson wanted to become president and JFK to be his vice president. JFK and his father were vying for the presidency and no way would they accept the second position. Meetings were being held all day and Matty was required to be present.

Matty had become friendly with then Gov. Hughes, who arranged to have a state trooper pick us up at the airport and bring us to the Hildebrand. On that particular day, I flew Matty to Trenton round trip three times and when we landed at Trenton, we were both exhausted. He decided to stay at the Hildebrand overnight but I had a morning obligation and had to return to Bowles Airport in Agawam.

Before departing, I checked by radio with the FAA Station in Newark and was assured that the weather on my route was favorable. The flight was uneventful until I arrived at the mountainous area over Torrington, Connecticut.

Unexpectedly, the airplane began to sound like a tympani drum and it was ear shattering! The plane was being pelted by hailstones the size of marbles and I had to resort to instrument flying. I was alone and it was scary but I had good control.

Eventually, I broke out of the storm and made a safe landing at Bowles Airport. The next morning, Charlie Lukas, the airport manager, called me and wondered how I was able to return and land during such a bad storm.

If Matty had remained with me on the return flight, it would not have been a passenger problem as he was an Air Force navigator during World War II. This was a day that I'll always retain in my memories.

MEMORIES OF EILEEN GRIFFIN

By Ann Martin Gibbons

Eileen Griffin and I both grew up on Governor Street. Eileen was a true profile in courage by opening the judiciary gate for women when she was appointed to be the first woman judge from Western Massachusetts and I was the second. What a tribute to Governor Street!

Eileen did not have an easy life. Despite the loss of a brother at a young age, a chronically ill sister and a sick mother to care for, Eileen persevered and earned a college degree and a subsequent law degree.

She worked as a secretary for Attorney General Paul Dever and when he became governor, he made Eileen a District Court Judge. She later became a Superior Court Judge. She was an amazing, focused, woman and an inspiration for so many other women of that era.

REFLECTIONS ON ANN MARTIN GIBBONS

Ann (Anna Mae) Martin Gibbons was born and raised on Hungry Hill on Governor Street. She graduated from Elms College, Clark University and earned a J.D. degree from Western New England Law School. After teaching chemistry at Regis College, Ann served as Holyoke City Solicitor in Holyoke and Treasurer of the Hampden County Bar Association. She was appointed to the bench in 1977 and became the Presiding Justice at Ware District Court ,where she implemented a new prototype for handling domestic violence through prevention and education.

In addition, she was a faculty member at the National Judicial College in Reno, Nevada; served as District Director of the National Association of Women Judges and was on the governor's select committee on judicial reform and other judicial education committees. She and her husband, Attorney Leonard Gibbons, were both recognized by the St. Thomas More Society which is a Catholic Lawyers Association. Ann came from a family of achievers. Her brother John P. became a priest and then a Monsignor and her sister Mary M. Walsh was a renowned educator in Springfield serving as a teacher, principal and assistant superintendent. Upon her retirement in the 1980s, the Sixteen Acres School was renamed for her.

Ann was a neighbor and friend of Eileen Griffin on Governor Street. She followed Eileen's lead by being the second woman to be appointed as a District Court Judge from Western Massachusetts. She was well-liked and respected by peers and court personnel alike. She was very supportive of each member of her court staff in Ware, whom she treated like an extended family. She and her Clerk Magistrate, Jim Bloom, were a model for other courts in the region. They managed a steady caseload fairly and evenly and were a very compatible team. Ann is an inspiring example of a woman being able to have it all, a distinguished career, a loving husband and mother of four children.

REFLECTIONS ON SISTER KATHLEEN KEATING

Kathleen Keating grew up on Nottingham Street on Hungry Hill, the youngest of four children of James and Mary Begley Keating. She attended Liberty School and Our Lady of Hope School. She graduated from Cathedral High School and Elms College before joining the Sisters of Saint Joseph. Advanced degrees include a master's degree from Villanova University and a doctorate from Fordham University.

Kathleen taught secondary schools for 11 years and was a faculty member at Elms for nine years. Her many activities include Chair of the National Assembly of Women religious, the National Women's Task Force of the Consultation on Church Union, President of the SSJ and Region I Chair of the Leadership Conference of Women Religious. She served as President of Elms College from 1994 to 2001.

Sister Kathleen credits her parents for making education a priority in their house and giving her a wonderful foundation in life upon which she was able to build. While there was always a scarcity of material goods, she and her siblings, Joan, Maureen and Geoffrey, reaped the benefits of unconditional love, a very rich faith and a value system imbued with gospel principles. Theirs was a childhood filled with grace and was truly, "the world's best start."

MEMORIES OF ELEANOR POWELL

By Murray Harris

My sister Florence was born in 1912, the same year as Eleanor Powell. When she was seven years old, my parents enrolled her in a dancing school on Worthington Street. The instructor was Ralph McKernan. Eleanor Powell was also a member of that same class.

Both were taught tap dancing, toe dancing and classic dance. At age 16, Florence was a professional dancer, performing at the Elks Club, the Masons and the Oaks Club on State Street.

Eleanor's family lived on Newbury Street and she attended Liberty School on Carew Street. My parents operated a market on Liberty Street. Mr. and Mrs. Powell were regular customers and they became friendly.

When Eleanor rocketed to prominence and became an international star, her tap dancing was an important ingredient in her success. I saw every one of her movies. Some movie stars changed their names. Eleanor proudly remained Eleanor Powell and her memory lingers on.

POLICEMEN FROM HUNGRY HILL
by Dan Keyes

For many years, there were more members of the Springfield Police Dept. who lived on Hungry Hill than in any other neighborhood in the city. Some of the ones I remember are as follows:

John Maloney	ChiefJohn Fleming
Eugene Maloney	Wickie Sears
Robert Maloney	Jerry Kane*
John Lyons	Chief Ed Kane*
Paul Fenton	Chief Bernard Kane*
Midge Reilly Deputy Chief	Jim Kane*
Dan Keyes	Captain Phil Kane*
Pat Fahey	* 5 Kane Brothers on force at same time
Jim Fahey	Tom Moriarty
Tom O'Connor	Pat Bowler
Tim Garvey	Bill Hogan
Tom Wynn	George O'Brien

Tom Keyes   Bill Marren

Bill Carney   John Long

Tim O'Connell   John Carney
(Boy cop)

HUNGRY HILL PRIESTS
By Dan Keyes

Manning	O'Connor (2)
Johnson	Callahan
Lohan	Wynn
Sears	Dowd
Murphy	(2)Keyes
Reilly	Burke
Brunton	Fennell
Scahill	Kennedy
Begley	Gaffney
Mesit	Martin
Loughran	Marchese

Hungry Hill Lawyers
By Dan Keyes

Ryan	Hanley
Tom O'Connor	Reilly
Bernard O'Connor	Tagliavini
Eileen Griffin	Harris
Ann Martin Gibbons	Foley
Keyes	Sypek

HUNGRY HILL'S GREEK COMMUNITY

GROWING UP GREEK

Hungry Hill was home to many Greek immigrants from the very early days. The Greeks and the Irish were very compatible and were good neighbors.

Peter and Tula Speliopoulos immigrated from Lagadia, Greece and originally settled in Greenfield. In 1925, they bought a two- family house on Nottingham Street in Springfield which is still in the family. At the time they purchased this house, Nottingham Street was unpaved and was known as Chicopee Road according to the deed. City maps from that period showed Chicopee Road running the length of Nottingham Street, stopping on Carew and picking up again on Newbury Street.

Louise Speliopoulos was born in this house and she and her three brothers grew up in the neighborhood and attended Liberty and Van Sickle schools. They worshiped at St. George Greek Orthodox Church which was then a small church on Patton Street. She and her brothers walked to Greek School there every day after school from 4 to 6 p.m. where they studied the Greek language and Greek history. A striking portrait of her great grandfather, George Peter Speliopoulos, in traditional Greek costume has a prominent place in her home. Though most of her friends are Irish, Louise is still fluent in the language and likes to socialize with Greek-speaking people so she won't lose this gift.

Shortly after his arrival in this country, Louise's father started his own business in downtown Springfield known as the New Bridge Luncheonette located on Vernon and Broadway, near the once well-known Honeymoon Hamburg. She recalls as a young girl, she helped out in the restaurant and brought coffee and doughnuts to the police station for the prisoners that had been arrested the night before.

Though they were totally Americanized, the Speliopoulos family kept many Greek traditions especially where food was concerned. Spanikopita, lamb and baklava were favorites in their household. Louise recalls that her brother, Phil, was a sickly child and couldn't tolerate cow's milk. Fortunately, they had a Greek neighbor, Mrs. Daras, who raised goats, so they were able to get fresh goat's milk for him.

The Greek Orthodox Church played an important role in the lives of local Greek families for weddings and funerals and other rites of passage. To this day, Louise is a member of St. George's Greek Orthodox Cathedral. She talked about the schism that occurred several years ago when a group of parishioners broke off from St. George's to form another Greek congregation in East Longmeadow called St. Luke's. Louise sometimes attends services there. She reminisced about the Orthodox Easter which, every four years, falls on the same day as the Christian Easter. The Greeks traditionally dye eggs red which signifies the blood of Christ. Also, a Greek tradition is to pick up a red egg and tap the egg that another person is holding, saying in Greek, *Christ is Risen.*

Faith Karamallis Perrault was brought up on Biella Street. Her parents, Tula and Harry, had three children, Elaine, George and Faith. Like most Greek families in the area, they belonged to St. George's Greek Orthodox Church in downtown Springfield. Faith and her siblings attended Liberty School and Van Sickle. Two days a week, after school, Faith and her siblings took the bus to St. George's for Greek School from 4 to 6 p.m. Education was stressed in most Greek families. This included Greek education for the purpose of keeping the language and history in the lives of their children. Though many of the Greek children could speak the language fluently, in Greek School they learned to write it as fluently.

Very prominent in their childhood, was membership in the St. George Olympians Drum Corp. From age 8, Faith was in the feeder or junior corps of younger siblings who were fed into the drum corps as they got old enough to participate. Faith was ten years old when she started marching with the Drum Corps. It was set up then that the boys played instruments and the girls were in the color guard and carried a flag or a rifle. They met for practice three times a week at places like Van Horn Park, the grounds at the Westinghouse and the Springfield Plaza. The parents were actively involved in the drum corps as committee members. The committee consisted of six sets of parents (the "daffy dozen") who got together on Friday nights along with their kids. The parents played cards and the kids hung out together. So the drum corps was a tightly knit community. The families went on trips together as well as competitions and parades. Drum Corps was a commitment through high school and even then, members stayed on as substitutes. This experience resulted in lasting friendships, not to mention the many marriages that came from drum corps membership. Faith met her husband in drum corps.

Faith talked about the differences in the Catholic and the Greek Orthodox rituals. When a child is baptized into the Greek Orthodox faith, they receive first communion and confirmation all at the same time. In the Catholic faith, there are three different ceremonies with many years between them. Also, to receive communion in the Orthodox church, you are obligated to fast from the night before, which used to be the case for Catholics. Previously, they fasted from dairy and meat for three days before receiving communion. One thing Faith always wished she could do was wear a lace doily on her head like her Catholic friends did when attending church. At their Orthodox service, hats were required. She pointed out that the word Orthodox means "original" and they kept most of the original traditions.

She recalls that food and the preparation of food was very important in Greek families. Holy Week in the past meant that her grandparents would come from New York and stay with them. Her two grandmothers would be in the cellar where they had a whole kitchen set up for cooking the traditional Greek dishes, dying the eggs red and making the Easter pastries, breads and Easter soup called Magrayitsa. Easter dinner was always lamb and they tried to use every part of the lamb. The soup consisted of the head of the lamb and the intestines with a lemon additive. They made their own filo dough, stretched it out on a table to let it dry and then cut it into squares for the baklava. Also, during Holy Week, they attended church every night.

Emmanuel "Manny" Rovithis, the owner and founder of Manny's TV & Appliance stores, was born on the Island of Crete. His father immigrated to this country first and then sent for his family. Manny was twelve years old when he arrived in his new country and his new home on Carew Street in the Hungry Hill section of Springfield. His parents, Demetrios and Maria, had five children; Manny, his brother Steven and three daughters, Stella, Evanne and Christina. Manny attended Liberty School and Van Sickle, which couldn't have been easy as he didn't speak English. Manny recalls that they had very good teachers who made it easier. He found the basic subjects to be the same as the ones they had in Greece.

From the time he landed in this country, Manny seemed to have a built-in entrepreneurial spirit and was willing to work hard. At age 14, he and Steve had a massive downtown paper route with 750 customers all along Main Street from the Paramount Theater to the Greek Church, which then consisted of numerous stores, restaurants and bars. At Christmas, he recalls that their tips were upwards of $2,000.

After that, the brothers had a hot dog cart. They worked late hours until the bars closed when they would do a huge business. After Van Sickle, Manny opted to go to Trade School (Putnam Vocational) which offered a course of study where you went to school for a week and then worked for a week in your chosen field. Manny took up electronics and got a job at the House of Television, where he worked for 12 years and laid the foundation for operating his own business.

Like most Greeks in the area, Manny and his family belonged to St. George's Orthodox Church. When he and his brother weren't working on their paper route and hot dog cart, they were involved with the St. George Olympians Drum Corps. He and his siblings did not attend Greek School as they were new arrivals and were already entrenched in the culture. His family still keeps the Greek traditions, including the food.

Manny represents another generation of Hungry Hill success stories. His head for business has served him well. From a paper route and hot dog cart, he has risen to being the owner of four appliance stores in the area. He speaks well of his Hungry Hill background and the many friends he made there. Even after he got married, he stayed in the neighborhood for awhile on Home Street.

The feedback I gathered from Greek residents and business owners on Hungry Hill was consistent. The Greek experience on Hungry Hill involved working hard, keeping their faith, willingly sharing their traditions and easily assimilating into a diverse neighborhood.

Efharistoomay! (we thank you) for being good neighbors and good friends and for adding so much to the neighborhood.

George Peter Speliopoulos patriarch
Speliopoulos Family Nottingham Street

HUNGRY HILL GREEK FAMILIES

Speliopoulos	Sarandes
Papadopoulos	Verrailes
Andrews	Krokidis
Delavorias	Karamallis
Daras	Rovithis
Lolas	Albanes
Hyfantis	Demos
Themistos	Hoontis
Ampolakis	Nikitas
Palapoulos	Demos
Katsounis	Agnos (St.James Ave)
Lamanis	Theocoles
Agnos (Corona St.)	Arthur Agnos became the mayor of San Francisco
Chaklis	Vakakis
Peros	Passidakis
Sumares	Trikas
Tougias	Carellas
Spano	Milidakis

Moritakis   Joanides

Pappas   Papadoulias

Note: This partial list of Greek families was compiled "word of mouth" from many former residents and my own personal knowledge. There were many others that I didn't know about or forgot about-who are included in spirit.

THE ITALIAN COMMUNITY

The Serras of Hungry Hill

The Serras were part of a large number of Italian families who date back to the early 1900s on Hungry Hill. Most of the Italians that settled on the hill were from Northern Italy. The Italians from the southern part of Italy were primarily located in the south end of Springfield. The Irish and Italian families on Hungry Hill got along famously. They shared their lives gladly and often. They traded at the same stores, went to the same doctors and worshiped at the same church. Though many Italians went to Our Lady of Hope Church, their kids were instructed in Christian Doctrine by an Italian priest from Mount Carmel Church every Friday after school.

The Serras were a large Italian family who all lived in the same section of Hungry Hill, on Nottingham, Wilbur, Clantoy and Hamlet Streets. John Serra and his sister Louise Laroche, are from Hamlet Street where they lived all their lives. Their father, Primo Serra, emigrated from Italy around 1906 when he was a young, single man. He left Italy with a price on his head due to his outspoken political views. He made his way across Northern Italy and France and boarded a ship in Le Havre and sailed to America. He had some friends in Springfield, where he stayed and he worked at a box shop in West Springfield for awhile. He then went back to Italy and married Albina Morisi. They stayed in Italy for a few years and had one child and were expecting another one when he talked her into coming to America. So, they left Italy with nothing but the clothes on their backs for the promise of a better life in a new country. Because of her pregnancy, the captain of the ship kindly gave Albina quarters near the center of the boat where there would be less rocking motion. On arrival at Ellis Island, Albina hid the fact that she was pregnant as she feared they would not allow her to enter the country. Her cousin Ida, on the same ship, had an infection in her eyes and they were very bloodshot. Albina thought quickly and told the Ellis Island officials that her cousin had been crying a lot because of leaving home, so she was allowed to enter.

John has great pride in his parents and the other people from Europe who made this country great. He likes to tell the story about the origin of the term "wop". According to popular belief, this term indicated "Without Papers" or "Without Passport". Until 1921, passports and visas were not required of immigrants entering the United States and their status was "wop.". This folklore has been disputed by some, including *Wikipedia* which states that the word "wop" was used before that time to describe a flamboyant Italian man.

The Serras had seven children in their family and lived next to the large Carey family with their ten children and a menagerie of barnyard animals. Hamlet Street was then a dirt road with open fields that extended to Nottingham Street and was often referred to as Carey's Farm or Carey's Cow Flop. Aggie Carey, one of the Carey daughters, had the job of moving the cow several times a day.

A big event those days was when Pat Leahy, an immigrant from Ireland, like Mr. Carey, came by to butcher a pig. He had a special tool that he used for this. As a boy, John Serra's job was to stir a large bucket of blood from the pig which was used to make blood sausage. Nothing was wasted; they even cooked the tail of the pig. Both the Serras and the Careys had huge gardens and grew most of their own food. Gardens were an integral part of the landscape in those days and pretty much a necessity. Peter Hogan allowed people who didn't have large yards to use his land on Liberty Street for vegetable gardens.

Primo made homemade wine—his family always had wine at the table. Italian kids had *vin cin* (diluted wine). Primo used zinfandel grapes from California and made about 150 gallons of wine a year-mostly muscatel, a sweet wine that Albina would sometimes use in cooking.

As kids on Hamlet Street, their world was pretty small. They would go to Mrs. Sear's store, known as the green store, which later became Demos' store. It was located at McBride and Nottingham Streets adjacent to the goat fields on Griffin Street. Another popular place for kids was the Lombard reservoir or Hallwrights. The actual spelling of the name is uncertain though John Serra believes the owner of the property lived near Armory and Liberty Streets and it might have been his family name.

During the Depression years, the field from Nottingham to Hamlet Street was used as a park area called Wilbur Bowl. It was run by Flop McCarthy and was used for football and baseball games. Eventually, it was sold to contractors who built houses there. Louise played third base on the girl's all-city softball team, which used Wilbur Bowl for their games.

One activity that John and his friends liked to do after church on Sundays was to go to the stable where St. Mary's Church is now located, where they were able to rent a horse for about 25 cents and take a ride, sometimes as far as Bircham Bend. Kay Belton, who lived on Kendall Street, kept her horse there.

Another Italian, Mr. Guidetti, lived on Nottingham Street, near Eddy Street and had a huge amount of land which he used for vegetable gardens. John Serra worked for him while he attended Van Sickle. He learned how to sprout the tomato plants in the cellar and transfer them to the greenhouse. Mr. Guidetti had cold frames with shades made out of tarpaper. John's job was to take the shades off when the sun was out and cover them at night. He also accompanied Mr. Guidetti and helped to deliver fruits and vegetables to regular customers. To this day, John is an accomplished gardener and can credit his green thumb and his love of growing things to Mr. Guidetti as well as his own family garden.

Through the years, the Italians had a positive influence on the Hungry Hill scene. For example, Galletti Brothers Market and Louie's Market, both on Liberty Street; Mrs. Cattachucci of Eddy Street who made tortellinis and sold them out of her house; Mr. Guidetti's gardens and the many winemakers, like Primo Serra and Tripoli Alovis from Nottingham Street. Also, the Marconi Club, complete with bocce courts, was built because the Hungry Hill Italians wanted a social club in their own neighborhood. That club was the setting for hundreds of weddings and other local events. To the Serras and other Italian *famillias* listed in this book as well as those included in spirit, for all you contributed to the neighborhood by your friendship and your culture –**SALUTE!!**

Italian Names on Hungry Hill

This is a partial list compiled by Dan Keyes, John Serra and myself. There were probably other Italian families on Hungry Hill who are not listed here but who are absolutely included in this tribute.

Bono	Ballardini
Fagoni	Facchini
Del Pozzo	Carpinelli
Guidetti	Palpani
Mandrala	Mazzoli
Biagetti	Nardi
Malvezzi	Pioggia
Vechiarelli	Palazzesi
Carpenelli	Gatti
Pajoli	Artoli
Mencarelli	Tebaldi
Christofori	Cavicchioli
Sarnelli	Cabrini
Zeo	Marasi
Tarozzi	Salemo

Tranghese	Martinelli
Gallerani	Ugolini
Manfredi	Catalucci
DelNegro	Cocchi
Catachucci	Accorsi
Baldarelli	Montinari
Fabbri	Violante
DeBonis	Valentine
Germani	Rossini
Cortelli	Lamborghini
Lacedonia	Stellato
Sarna	D'Ambrosio
Sapelli	Berani
Rossini	Galletti
Bruno	Balboni
Zona	Bercelli
Mastroianni	Pandolfi
Vancini	Cassanelli
Vadini	Restanio
Restanio	Pepe

Govoni	Rosati
Ruggieri	Chicketti
Guidoni	Bellucci
Tagliavini	Roncalato
Lambert	Small (English translation)
Marchetti	Maggi
Marino	Pasquini
Balegano	Pasqualini
Cicerchia	Sabatini
Morisi	Cardinale
Bussolari	Palpini
Berte	Alessandri
Scaglarini	Zanetti
Alovis	Serra
Montesi	Collina
Valenti	Petri

Being Jewish on
Hungry Hill

BEING JEWISH ON HUNGRY HILL

Murray Harris was born and bred on Hungry Hill and was part of a small enclave of nine Jewish families who lived in the neighborhood at that time. The Jewish community included the Blakey Family on Liberty Street; the Horowitz family on Grover Street, who had a small store in their house; the Wolfe family on Langdon Street; the Berlin family on lower Carew Street near the Shriner's hospital; the Kazin family, who had a pharmacy on the corner of Armory and Liberty Streets and lived on Carew Street opposite Penacook Street; the Weinberg and Lavin families of Stafford Street; and the Kantor family of Lexington Street. who operated Kantor's Market on Carew Street near Bartlett Street. Murray's family ran Harris Market for 45 years, which was on Liberty Street near Grover and Cleveland Streets and they lived in the apartment upstairs.

There were six children in the family and almost all of them were trained musicians: Milly, a graduate of one of the first classes at Bay Path Institute, now known as Bay Path College; Florence, who was a professional tap, toe, ballet and classic dancer with Eleanor Powell, the movie star; Seymour, who was Matty Ryan's first assistant district attorney; Murray, an accomplished musician and pilot; Polly. who earned a Master's degree in social work from UConn and the youngest son, Earl, who, tragically, became incapacitated at a very young age due to severe head injuries from an accident.

The children attended Armory Street School. In keeping with their Jewish faith, Murray and his brother went to Hebrew school three nights a week until their bar mitzvah at the Jewish synagogue on Sharon Street. In addition, the Harris family had a deep respect and a solid friendship with Our Lady of Hope Church on a non-religious level. In the early days, Murray's father delivered groceries in a horse and wagon. He kept the horse in a barn that he rented on Webster Street. On one occasion, a dog scared the horse and the wagon went into a tree. Mr. Harris was injured and was laid up for a few weeks, leaving his wife with several small children and a business to run.

Mrs. Harris went to Father Cruse, the pastor of Our Lady of Hope Church, for help. Father Cruse sent two men every day to help Mrs. Harris at no cost to her. When Mr. Harris got out of the hospital, he and his wife went to visit Father Cruse and made a donation to the church for the help they received. His parents and Father Cruse shared a mutual respect and became good friends.

From that time on, Father Cruse arranged to purchase the rectory groceries from Harris Market. Also, when the family spent a day at the beach, he let them use the parking and shower facilities at his place in Ocean Beach, Connecticut. The Harris family regularly attended the minstrel shows at the old Lady of Hope Church. Another fond memory of Our Lady of Hope was watching their neighbors walking to Mass dressed up in their Sunday best, a tradition that no longer exists, with very few exceptions.

Murray remembers when the Martin Brunton home stood where the Liberty Branch Library is now. Every winter, he had the job of shoveling their sidewalk from Kendall Street to the Liberty Café, the circular driveway to their backyard and under the clothesline for 25 cents. The house was moved to Kendall Street when the new library was built.

Murray was very musically inclined and at age 11, took trumpet lessons from Chet Griffin, a professional musician who played first trumpet for the Springfield Symphony. He took two busses to get to Chet's house on Florence Street. As the Depression worsened and money got tighter, Murray's mother notified Chet that they would have to stop the lessons, which were one dollar, but Chet insisted that the lessons continue and they could pay him something whenever they could. So Murray continued his trumpet lessons and eventually played in the Classical High School band.

At age 16, Murray had his own orchestra consisting of Wilfred Berard from Freeman Terrace on the piano; two saxophone players, Alphonse Khachuba, who went on to play with Glenn Miller and Milton Kitchener whose family owned Kitchener's Department Store in Indian Orchard; Murray and Dino Gillette were on trumpets, Dino's brother Elliot was on drums, Bobby Kuhn from Carew Street played the banjo and Jackie Kelleher played the violin. They rehearsed every Tuesday night and Murray's parents would provide snacks for the musicians.

The Harris family had a large circle of friends and neighbors. Murray had a lifelong friendship with Dan Keyes and Matty Ryan which began in kindergarten at Armory Street School in 1921. After Armory, they were classmates in the first class at the newly built Van Sickle Junior High School and played baseball and soccer together. Both Dan Keyes and Matty were excellent athletes and tough competitors.

This section of Hungry Hill had a very eclectic population in those days who practiced the adage "live and let live." Mrs. Harris was Jewish and had immigrated from Poland. Grover Street was mainly Italian, the Del Pozzos, the Bonos, the Ristanos and the Tuccis, among others.

Cleveland Street was mostly Irish—the Currans, the Fitzgeralds, the Cahills, the Mannings, the Foleys, the Potters, the McLaughlins, the Leonards, the Kellehers-- a very musical family who ran the Cleveland Street theater in their garage; the MacDonalds, who had a blacksmith shop in their yard; the Footman family with daughters who looked like movie stars and the Flynn family whose son was a gifted artist. There was "Tip" Appleby from Clantoy Street;" Pie" McNulty of Woodmont Street, "Gin bottles" O'Connell of Hastings Street; "Waggin Ears" Cohen; "Congo" Keyes and "Wiggie" Biglon of Cherrelyn Street; the Rogers brothers of Grover Street, who were early motorcyclists; Jim and Margaret Harrigan of Clantoy Street, (Jim was a popular detective on the police department); Willum Garvey of Phoenix Street, who became a state trooper; and Hubbie McGovern of Roy Street whose mother baked homemade bread that she delivered in a small wagon during the Depression years. Sadly, Hubbie died at a very young age when a makeshift raft he built capsized on Hogan's ice pond.

Murray also has fond memories of the Shea family who had six kids, Tom, who became a keen political strategist, Mary, Neely, Tossie, John and Bart. Then there were the Sullivans, the Mansfields, the Sears family, Jimmy O'Connell, known as the "the boy cop" for his work with young boys, the Milbiers, the O'Neils, the Capkos, Stash Ciechanowicz, Frank Donovan and his wife, Marie Carey from Hamlet Street, the Haggertys and the Curleys.

One very colorful figure, well-known around Bottle Park, was Tom Pollard, who lived on Van Buren Street and was a regular customer at the Harris Market. Tom was a highly regarded horse trainer known throughout the United States. He had a small barn in his back yard where Murray often visited to watch him train the horses, a skill that he learned in his native Ireland. Last but not least, there was Hockitty Graves, who seemed to be known by everyone on Hungry Hill.

Many small businesses thrived over the years on this stretch of Liberty Street. In addition to Harris Market, there was Rice and Murphys, Papageorge's Barber Shop, Peter Loughran's market, Vezina's Drug Store, Liberty Bakery, the Liberty Theater, the Liberty Hardware store at the corner of Liberty and Kendall, (operated by the Malaguti family) and Bussolari's ice cream and candy store on Libcar Street. When the A&P opened, Murray's parents became friendly with the store manager, Jack Quinn. Many times, if an item wasn't stocked in the Harris Market, Jack Quinn would provide it from the A&P at wholesale rates.

Murray looks back on his experience of growing up Jewish in a Christian/Catholic arena as a very positive one without any type of prejudice. As both parents worked hard in their market, they always had a live-in housekeeper to run the house and take of the children. Murray recalls Mrs. Simpson, a lady from Ireland who would sit him on her lap and sing the "Irish Lullaby" to him. Many years later, when he entered naval flight school as a cadet, he needed three references. They were all from the neighborhood and none of them were Jewish: Danny Brunton, Raoul Vezina of Vezina's Drug Store on Liberty Street and Father Cruse from Our Lady of Hope.

After 8 years in the military, Murray worked at several jobs ranging from a swimming instructor at a boys camp in Maine to a program director for the Burroughs Foundation in Boston to a hardware business with his brother Seymour in Springfield and finally, a bank manager for the Chicopee Savings Bank. He kept his flying license and had his own plane which he kept at Bowles Airport in Agawam.

To the Harris Family and the other Jewish residents and merchants of Hungry Hill such as the Kazins, the Kantors, Jack and Dave Goldberg and Louie Zointz, thank you all for personifying the Jewish phrase *L'Chaim* (to life) by your contributions to the life and flavor of the neighborhood.

Sadly, Murray Harris passed away in February of this year as this book went to press. He was a contributor to the now defunct Hungry Hill Magazine as well as a regular contributor to the Ludlow Register and the Republican. He was a wealth of information and knew hundreds of people by name. He will be missed by many.

A Kid's Life
on Hungry Hill
50 years of growing

LIFE OF A HUNGRY HILL KID - 1920S AND 1930S

By Dan Keyes

As kids, Hungry Hill was our playground. There were no "gangs" as we know them today. Each neighborhood had its own athletic teams. The Blackstones came from the area around Liberty and Phoenix Streets and held football practice on the city lots located on Liberty Street adjacent to St. Benedict's Cemetery. After World War II, the site was occupied by the headquarters of American Legion Post 430 and later by a food and produce outlet which has since been replaced by sundry smaller commercial establishments. In addition, there were the Acorns from the Van Horn area, the Bluebirds from East Springfield, the American AC from the Freeman Terrace region around Hasting and Stockman Streets and the Wilburs from the old campgrounds. They were rivals but never enemies. Whenever violence was resorted to in order to settle a disagreement, it was usually by way of a fistfight between individuals. There were no guns or knives or deadly weapons of any description nor was there ever any intention of inflicting serious bodily injury.

On Cleveland Street, a family by the name of Kelleher owned a large multi-car garage made of cement blocks which, for all practical purposes, was big enough for use as a warehouse. On Saturday afternoons, the building was converted into a quasi-movie theater which was patronized by a standing room audience of the Hill's adolescents. Admission was five cents and payment thereof entitled the youthful patron to a free piece of fudge. A large screen was mounted on a raised platform at the front of the building, with folding chairs set up to accommodate about 200 people. The program invariably consisted of three motion pictures: a comedy, a serial movie, and a western or cowboy movie. All of the movies shown at the Cleveland were silent. Sound movies or "talkies" didn't become universal until the late 20s or early 30s. Any dialogue or conversation was scripted across the bottom of the screen and was dubbed in to coincide with the movement of the actor's lips. Usually a piano player sat at the front of the theater just below the screen and played whatever tunes were deemed appropriate to the activities being portrayed. The Cleveland was our Saturday refuge, especially during the winter months, until the arrival of the more modern Liberty Theater on Liberty Street around 1930.

The Liberty Theater was located across from Cleveland Street about a one-minute walk from where we lived on Grover Street and 30 seconds from where we would later live on Phoenix Street. It was there that I saw for the first time a motion picture with sound. We never ran out of dishes as every Friday was "dish night" when every female adult patron received a complimentary piece of china.

Summer was baseball, purely and simply baseball. If you weren't at the main diamond at Van Horn Park on time, you were shut out. No favoritism was shown to anyone, including players of superior ability. There was also sandlot baseball teams and the Triple A league which comprised teams representing different industries and business establishments in the Springfield area and featured many players of exceptional talent.

I remember vividly a game in which I participated which was against the Trojans, a 12-14 team from the Ruth Elizabeth playground area who had traveled halfway across the city to play Our Lady of Hope on a Sunday afternoon. The pitcher for the Trojans was a 14- year-old kid by the name of Vic Raschi, who, after his discharge from the service at the end of World War II had an outstanding career with the New York Yankees, playing in several World Series. Raschi threw a three-hit shutout against Our Lady of Hope that day but most noteworthy, the score card showed that two of the three hits were by second baseman Keyes. So what if they were "bleeders"?

Summertime was also marbles and a week's vacation at the Boy's Club Camp in Brimfield. We swam at Hogan's pond on upper Liberty Street, but an even more popular swimming retreat was the makeshift BAB (bare-assed beach) one of which was deep in the lower woods just off Freeman Terrace, and another in the wooded area behind Armory Street School. BAB was another name for the "old swimming hole" crudely constructed by damming up a brook with mud and logs, thereby creating a pool of water in which we could swim on the blazing days of summer. We played jack-knife, relievio, buck-buck, and a myriad of other kid games. Marbles was a special favorite. Marbles became especially popular in our area when a local boy, Howard "Dutchy" Robbins, won the national championship in Atlantic City in the early 1930s.

As I recount these recollections from the ever-lengthening corridors of memory, many of the things I remember and cherish the most are the amorphous sounds and sights and smells of days long gone. Lying in bed at night, half asleep, listening to the mournful whistle of the train as it raced into the night only a few hundred yards from our home; the clip-clop sound of horses' hooves against the pavement and the clinking rattle of bottles as the milkman made his house-to-house deliveries in the pre-dawn hours; the family gatherings in the kitchen; the sound of laughter on a cold winter's night when the rest of the house was closed off to preserve the heat from the kitchen stove; the exchange between siblings, sometimes heated, but never hateful, induced undoubtedly, in part, by prolonged proximity; the smell of my mother's homemade bread; the interchange between my mother and her cronies as they gathered in the parlor of our home on Wilbur Street on Saturday nights to talk about people and events in a language that only "green horns" understood; the sounds of the church bell in Our Lady of Hope tower every evening at 6 o'clock, reminding us of the Angelus; the clanging sound of the trolley; the voices of youth floating across the dusk from every corner of Van Horn Park on a warm summer evening; the stillness and solemnity in church on a Saturday afternoon when confessions were being heard with at least ten pews filled with penitents at Father Lacey's confessional and no one on the side of the church where the pastor sat.

As I look back from the vantage point of old age to those years of pristine simplicity that defined our innocence and reflect on the way we were and on the in-between years that have flown so swiftly and brought us to where we are, I paraphrase an old verse I heard many years ago:

Time, father time, turn back in thy flight,

And make me a boy again just for tonight.

Daniel M. Keyes, Jr.

THE SUMMER OF '43

Growing up in the 1940s on Hungry Hill

By Robert Welch

It has been stated more than once that to reminisce is to be sentimental. Being guilty of that I cannot help but reflect on what it was like when we were kids growing up on Hungry Hill.

The day would start with the five of us, Billy Sullivan, Juny and Andy "Squirt" DeDeurwaerder, Jimmy McNamara and myself, making our way to Hogan's Pond behind Van Sickle. There we would build a raft using boards from the abandoned ice house. When completed, we would row out to the center of the pond, challenging the gang from the Judson Street area, "Bones" Martin, "Brother" Dan, Tommy Manning, Joe Nihill, Joe Labelle and others whose names now escape me.

At one time, I had the misfortune to step on a rusty nail, later to find myself limping with a sore swollen foot. In those days, a doctor was a stranger and penicillin was not available. Reluctant to tell my mother, I sought my father's advice. His West Kerry knowledge of medicine was limited and it was usually the same compassionate response. "Don't worry, it will go away." And do you know, he was right! The swelling eventually receded, however, I still carry the scar. After completing our raft skirmishes, it was then a further journey to the Springfield Airport.

Here we knew every aircraft by name. I can still visualize the Beechcraft, Cessna, Aeronaca and, of course, the venerable Piper Cub. To witness a Stearman or Waco firing up those large radial engines was a sight to behold. What power! Smoking rumbling, coughing and eventually developing into that rhythmic roar!

Leaving the airport, we then took a trip to the sandbanks, behind the plaza. It would start out as an innocent push and soon develop into a real "King of the Hill" battle. Those sandbanks were steep and by rights, someone should have broken some bones. However, we managed to survive.

Heading for home, a skinny dip in the pond was a requirement. Our clothes were neatly stacked into a bundle in anticipation of being chased by Paul Hogan on horseback. If at any time he would gain on us, we always had a lookout posted and we would split up and escape through the woods on familiar trails. There were times when we had to stop and put on some clothes as we neared civilization. This could prove to be embarrassing if anyone was using the playground behind Van Sickle.

As we made our way homeward, we visited the victory gardens between Savoy Avenue and Eddy Street. Here we happened upon Hockity Greaves picking apples and loading them into a shopping bag. When he wasn't looking, we grabbed the bag and threw the apples at him. He could not give us much of a chase as the poor man appeared to be older than dirt. His looks alone would frighten you.

A few days later he would be banging on our front door. My mother always called him by his first name which was Frank. I always managed to keep out of sight, not wanting to be identified as one of the rowdys from the day before. She would buy six apples for a nickel. Poor Hockity would claim that he picked them himself. He did, off the ground, they were all "drops."

The social scientists of today have tried to convince us that we as kids lived in an isolated world. We were never blessed with video games, computers or had the opportunity to sit in front of a TV for hours like robots.

Those innocent years of childhood have somehow slipped away. To be a 12-year old "bred and buttered" on Hungry Hill was the best of times! We missed nothing and escaped very little.

GROWING UP ON HUNGRY HILL 1950'S

By Robert "Wimpy" Lynch

We spent most of our time at Hogan's Pond. In the winter, we played hockey and in the summer, we built rafts from scrap lumber and poled our way around the pond. One day there was a huge hole in the dam. It was five feet in diameter and about ten feet deep. We thought it would make a great cave hut. The next day we brought shovels to shape beds in our new cave. When we arrived, we found that the cave was gone. Fortunately for us, it had collapsed during the night as we would have been killed had it happened during the day.

If we weren't at Hogan's we were at Hall-wrights (Horize). This was the land from the end of Clantoy Street to the railroad tracks. It had a reservoir with a brick chimney in the middle. The Murphy brothers bought an old Dodge for ten dollars which they left there. Anyone could drive it. I still remember riding on the back bumper. This is where many of us learned how to drive. As we got older and discovered beer, Horize became the place to drink beer and sing Irish songs all afternoon.

There was a hobo camp there. We were not supposed to go near it which made it more fascinating. We would dare each other to see how close we could go to the camp. When they left, we would explore their campsite. They ate a lot of Dinty Moore beef stew.

The railroad tracks provided a lot of entertainment. A favorite activity was hopping freight trains. We would run beside the train and grab the ladder and swing onto it. We would climb to the top of the box cars and jump from one to another. When we got to the Memorial Golf course, we would get off. Usually, the train was going faster than we could run so the dismount resulted in tumbling ass over teakettle! Sometimes we put pennies on the track and have the train flatten them.

Another activity was standing on the tracks with our backs to the oncoming train. There were four tracks. The passenger trains were usually on track one. We stood on track four and the first person to turn around was a chicken. With a steam engine blaring its whistle and roaring at us at high speed, it was impossible not to turn around!

Then, we discovered girls and the Friday night dances in the Van Sickle gym. The girls lined one wall and the boys had the other wall. When the music started, the boys would make the long walk across the floor and ask a girl to

dance. If she refused, the boy had to walk back –
it was the ultimate embarrassment! Dotty Young
taught me how to dance. Two steps to the right
followed by two to the left. Gramps Arsenault
did drum solos – he was really good! After the
dance, we went to the pizza shop. The alterna-
tive was the Family Circle Restaurant where an
ice cream sundae cost a quarter.

The Liberty Theater was the best place to
go with a girl. Two feature films and a cowboy
serial was standard. The serial ended with the
cowboy in a dire situation. You had to go back
the next week to see if he got out of the predica-
ment.

Other hangouts were Bottle Park and Friendly's. Also, we played football and baseball for
Lady of Hope and East Springfield. When we
played the South End, there was always the
chance of an after-game fight. Lake Lorraine
was another attraction. We hitchhiked to the
lake. When were short on funds, we would go
to Bums Beach and swim across the lake to the
Knights of Columbus Beach.

Turning 16 expanded our world. Drive-in
movies became the most popular date. Once
again, Horize was added to our hangout list. On
Saturdays, we got one of the older guys to buy
us a case of beer if we gave him a six- pack. We

would sit on the hoods of our cars and sing Irish rebel songs.

Hungry Hill was a moment in time. Geographically, it's still there but the way of life that it represented has vanished into memory.

LIFE OF A HUNGRY HILL KID IN THE 1960S

By Mark Morris

When my sister Joan asked me for a perspective on growing up in the 1960s and early 70s, my first thought was of Bob Dylan when pundits labeled him "the spokesman of his generation." While it's presumptuous to even make the comparison, I will humbly attempt to serve as a spokesman in a much smaller and friendlier forum.

I was too young in the early 1960s to remember anything except enormous events like the JFK assassination and even that was just confusing. I knew something bad had happened on that Friday, and yet I couldn't understand why Colonel Clown's Three Stooges Show wasn't on Channel 30 that Saturday morning. As the days and weeks went on, it became clearer to me that the president had been killed and our country was in heavy mourning. My mother preserved the special issues of *Life* and *Look* magazines by keeping them under the cushions of the den couch.

Recollections become more detailed as I think back on the mid-60s when I was 9-10 years old. Though I grew up in a working class family, my friends and I had enormous wealth that we couldn't appreciate at the time. We had the freedom of unsupervised play and plenty of room to exercise our bodies and our imaginations.

My parents intentionally built their house on Laurence Street so we could easily walk to both Liberty School and Van Sickle Junior High. I don't remember much about school activities, but the times hanging out with my friends Curt Fennyery and Dave Boris as well as, my cousins Lori and Candy Cabey, are memories that play like scenes from a favorite old movie.

An empty lot to the left of my house served as a multi-purpose field for various sports, games of tag and a stage for whatever make-believe play we invented. The street in front of the field served as the diamond for baseball soccer- a kickball game that loosely followed baseball rules. Home plate was a manhole cover in the middle of the street which was also home base for kick the can, the hide-and-seek game we favored.

A double lot thick with trees sat behind my house and provided the setting for various other adventures and a second stage for our imaginations. If you cut through the woods and walked across Middle Street, you would find a much larger field with high grass and small patches of woods. My brothers and sisters referred to it as "the goat field" but we didn't. With about five or six blueberry bushes we called it "the blueberry patch!" I often picked blueberries with the premise of giving them to my mother to bake muffins. Those good intentions, along with the berries, usually ended up in a bowl of milk with sugar sprinkled on top. Though she always agreed to do it, my mother seemed to understand that she would never be on the hook for actually baking something with my blueberry haul.

One common way we earned money was to cash in the deposit on soda bottles. Because they were refilled many times, the old glass bottles were thick and heavy. You only had to have five or six bottles to really cash in on those nickel deposits. My favorite soda back then was Country Club "California Orange." I was fascinated that Country Club Soda (which I perceived as a big shot company) was actually based in Springfield and not in some other state like Coke and Pepsi.

It was common to redeem the bottles and spend the proceeds at Joe's Variety Store, a tiny place on Carew Street directly across from Liberty School. It was a true "convenience store" before that term was invented. The sign above the door featured a Coke logo on each end and "Joe's Variety" spelled out in light green letters. Coca Cola provided this type of sign for hundreds of stores in our area and it was as familiar and effective as a stop sign.

Most of the time a woman named Cora ran the store. The namesake of the store was an elderly man and I remember seeing him there only once or twice. His son Joe Jr. (whom everyone called Little Joe) also worked at the store, usually on weekends.

Most of our business was conducted at the penny candy counter. Nonpareils, squirrel nut brand candy, wax lips, wax bottles with liquid inside, red licorice, coins, candy dots on strips of paper, we had them all! Most of the time, Cora would wait for us to contemplate which candies we desired. Occasionally, she would be short with us if other customers came in. Little Joe, on the other hand, was always impatient with us. I can still hear his signature nasal twang, a terse *"hairrry up!"* as we agonized how we would spend three cents.

Looking back, it's funny how no one ever questioned the unsanitary practice of Cora and Joe handling money and then counting out unwrapped pieces of candy on top of the glass counter where all sorts of business was conducted. There was no hand sanitizer, no hand washing, no gloves and no one got sick!

As an adult living in Feeding Hills, I don't have the intimate knowledge of my neighborhood that I had as a kid on Laurence Street. In those days, I knew all the shortcuts to get to adjacent streets and was familiar with every square inch of every neighbor's yard, because I often played in or walked through all of them.

All this nosing around in other people's yards sometimes led to puzzling discoveries. One day while playing in a neighbor's yard, I made an innocent find when I lifted the cover off a metal trash can (we often used the covers as shields in our sword fights). Right on top, separate from the bundled trash, sat an empty pint-size bottle of whiskey. I was confused because my Dad bought whiskey by the "fifth," a larger, more practical size to buy when you were entertaining guests. So, why would this person buy a pint bottle that wouldn't serve many people? I naively assumed that everyone bought booze for the same reason. It wasn't until years later, after this neighbor died and we heard rumors about an alcohol problem that my discovery made sense.

It was hard to notice how much the world was changing because I was also growing and changing as a person. My circle of friends expanded to other streets; Bill Wynne on Nottingham Street, Russ Frodema from Cabot Court, Mike Pandolfi on Biella Street and Jim Balboni on Carew Street. One common thread among all my friends was music. We lucked out on timing because the music of the 60s and early 70s served as our soundtrack. It was an amazing time for music and still accounts for most of my CD and iTunes collections.

Whether it was music, social change or technology, my generation was often right there to witness the twilight of the old ways and the adaptation of the new. The world outside the friendly confines of Laurence Street was undergoing an incredible transformation with both good and bad results.

Two of the Cabey brothers served in Vietnam. Tim joined the Marines and Buddy served in the Army. At the height of the war, many returning soldiers were greeted with scorn. Not so on Laurence Street! To greet Buddy, my sister Cheryl painted a sign on a four-foot by eight-foot piece of plywood, adorned with a picture of Beetle Bailey that read "Welcome Home Buddy!" My Uncle Bill proudly installed it in front of the Cabey house, where it stood long after Buddy returned home.

As the old saying goes, the only constant is change. As we grew older, all the woods and fields where we spent so many of our days became filled in with houses. As kids, we had the luxury to walk to school unsupervised. By the late 70s parents dutifully waited at bus stops with their kids who now rode across town for school.

As the "spokesman" for my generation, I will say one thing for certain: life on Laurence Street was a privilege I can appreciate only now, years later and decades removed. Our parents cared for us without hovering. We were allowed to play freely and stretch our imaginations in a million directions. We never worried about our safety and in this life, that's as good as it gets.

Neighborhood Notes and Nostalgia

FIFTY YEARS OF NOTES AND NOSTALGIA

"Hungry Hill was full of people and excitement, small houses, large families, tons of kids, churches full every weekend. It was a time of innocence and a time of change"...........
Richard Sypek

Alvin Street

Jim and Peg Sullivan, long-ime residents of Alvin Street on Hungry Hill, have been local radio personalities for 40 years on the *Irish Hours* program. They are well-known on Hungry Hill and have received recognition many times for their role in promoting Irish culture in the community.

Armory Street

Murty Reilly was a young man of 20 when he made a hasty departure from County Mayo, Ireland in 1920. He was part of the resistance movement against British occupation and a known IRA sympathizer. At that same time, as their sisters were leaving for America, other young men of 20 in Dingle, in the southwest of Ireland, were smuggling guns to be used when needed against the British troops in their town. A sister of the men from Dingle met and married the young man from Mayo and they started their new life on Armory Street in the Hungry Hill section of Springfield. Stories of patriots on both sides of the family resulted in the passing of the torch to one of Murty's sons, who gravitated towards the law and eventually became attorney general of Massachusetts. He, like his ancestors, was committed to preserving individual rights and liberties.

Border Street

Quiet little Border Street was the childhood home of an internationally acclaimed classical guitarist. Bernard Hebb lived at 37 Border Street, one of several houses on the street that his maternal grandfather, John A. Guynup had built that were occupied by Guynup relatives. Bernie attended Liberty School. His family moved to another state for his junior high and high school years.

He studied guitar in Austria and pursued a career path of performing and teaching classical guitar in over 14 countries. Bernie currently lives in Germany where he records and teaches his signature classical guitar.

Carew Street

Theresa Conway Balboni was a kid during World War II when her father, Joe, served as the civil defense warden for upper Carew Street and the side streets. During "blackouts," Joe had the job of checking each house in the neighborhood to make sure they complied with the rules. Joe also held first aid classes for neighbors and Theresa was the "victim" on whom everyone practiced making splints and bandaging until she could hardly move from the amount of bandages wrapped around her.

Drexel Street

Tom Shea of Drexel Street was a vital political force or more accurately, an enforcer who knew how to get things done. Tom had the power of persuasion, especially when it came to politics. He often hosted visiting pols, wining and dining them and delegating family members to chauffer them around Springfield. He was able to rally campaign workers even if they didn't want to work on a campaign but, amazingly found themselves involved. The late Judge Jim Landers called Tom the "gun" in political campaigns. Tom was always willing to use his political ties to help others.

Tom led Springfield's St. Patrick's Day Parade Committee for many years. His fundraising efforts for the parade were legendary. He was voted a member of the Holyoke Parade Committee's board of directors in 1958, making him the first board member from outside the city.

In 1973, he received the Gallivan Award and in 1984 he was the first out-of-towner to receive the O'Connell award.

Besides politics, one of his great passions was organizing the County Cork Reunion. His father emigrated from County Cork and Tom was fiercely proud of his heritage. The reunion was usually held in New York and was always well attended. One of Tom's last reunions included actress Maureen O'Hara.

Denton Circle

Rosemarie Tarozzi Pickett has fond memories of Sunday mornings after Mass when her father Victor, his brother Joe, Guy Veccharelli, "Skits" Rowe, Butch Dabrowski and various others gathered for their weekly "communion." This consisted of stopping on each floor of their three family house before Sunday dinner for spirits and conversation.

Rose recalls Denton Circle as being a virtual United Nations with Italian, Portugese, Polish, Lebanese, Greek, Russian, French and English families to name a few.

Eddy Street

Clare and John Sypek's four sons, John, Richard, Steve and Tom recall growing up on Eddy

Street, where they had their very own "Boston Garden" hockey rink in the sixties.

Richard Sypek has fond memories of yearly competitions with the Heaps and the Currans as to who would build the best hockey rink in their backyard. This involved going around the neighborhood in search of old doors and pieces of plywood. The Sypek rink was the entire length and width of their yard. Lights were strung from the upstairs bedroom across the entire backyard and tied up to a big oak tree. Their locker room was in the cellar which was a bunch of old folding chairs and some pieces of carpet.

Every winter day was the same routine, Liberty School, then Joe's Variety or Tony's Spa for a coke and chips. Then, after the paper route, supper and doing the dishes in teams of two, they rushed downstairs to get ready for a night of hockey. The lights were on and they made their way out of the hatchway onto the rink which shone like glass on cold winter nights. It was easy to envision yourself as Bobby Orr or Phil Esposito entering Boston Garden for hours of hockey. They were joined by the Heaps, the Currans, the Obergs and Nashvilles. They stayed on the ice until their mother flashed the lights. That was the signal to end the game and start cleaning the rink. Cleaning involved shoveling the ice, sweeping it clean and watering it every night.

Classical High and Cathedral High School got many of their hockey players from backyard rinks on Hungry Hill as well as the ponds at Van Horn Park.

John Sypek sums up life on Eddy Street in two words: sports and friends. He comments on the number of children on their end of Eddy Street, 57 kids in 13 houses. The games never stopped! In spring and summer, it was wiffle ball and base-ball in the back yards or on the street and touch football in the fall. The sewer covers were bases for the baseball games and telephone poles were the end zone markers for football games. If the hockey rinks were completed before it snowed, they were used for street hockey using tennis balls.

Steve Sypek wouldn't change a thing about his childhood on Eddy Street. He recalls sleepovers and eating peanut butter and fluff sandwiches at various neighbor's houses. Every house seemed to have an open door and you always felt welcome there. He loved growing up having wiffle ball and street hockey games right outside the door.

Tom Sypek's best memories of Eddy Street are about the meaning of family. He thinks back in amazement at how trusting everyone was on his street. They never had house keys growing up and if the door was locked you could borrow a skeleton key from any neighbor and it would open your door.

All of the Sypek brothers agree that they were blessed with hard-working, loving parents who instilled by example, a strong work ethic, the importance of family and of aiming high. They look back on Eddy Street as a neighborhood of great families and a true melting pot.

Glenham Street

George Littlejohn is the son of Scotch immigrants. His father, Tom Littlejohn, played soccer in Dundee, Scotland and was offered a job and lodging in the U.S. if he would play for an American team in Quincy, MA. He jumped at the chance to come to America where his team went as far as the national finals. He worked in the Fore River Ship Yard in Quincy. He met his wife Jemima, also an immigrant from Scotland. They moved to Springfield where George was raised on Glenham Street and then Sherbrooke.

George recalls that he and a few cohorts were known as "ruffians" mainly because they constantly got into trouble. At one point, he and Freddy Johnson were going to be sent to Shirley, MA to reform school. Thanks to the times and the number of people willing to get involved, this didn't happen. Out of the blue, Rev. Fowler of East Congregational Church in East Springfield came forth and asked the judge if he would assign the boys to his summer camp at Little Alum Lake rather than send them to Shirley. They would have to work all summer but they would have a place to stay and three meals a day. They gladly took him up on his offer and had a great summer.

George tells a Hungry Hill love story! He attended Liberty School and, from kindergarten on, was friends with Eleanor Linnehan of Phoenix Terrace. They knew each other all through school until George joined the Air Force. For a short time, he was stationed at Westover Air Force Base and became reacquainted with Eleanor, who he ended up marrying. This was a precarious merger of two families on opposite ends of the spectrum – his father was a 32nd Degree Mason and Eleanor's father was in the Knights of Columbus. Despite this, George and Eleanor had over 50 wonderful years together and had five children and 9 grandchildren.

Governor Street

Retired District Court Judge Ann Martin Gibbons credits the late Judge Eileen Griffin as a true profile in courage by opening the gate for women judges. Eileen was the first woman judge to be appointed from Western Mass. to the District Court. Judge Gibbons was the second and they were both from Governor Street! She later became a superior court judge for many years. She was very much a woman ahead of her time.

One of Judge Gibbons' fondest memories is the gang that hung out on the corner of Carew and Armory at Leo's Van Horn Spa every Sunday morning after Mass at Our Lady of Hope. The stores on the corner at that time consisted of Van Horn Spa, a barber shop, Ma Bouchard's Dough-nut shop, Mullane's Drug Store, Schmerhorn's Fish Market, First National Food Store and fur-ther down Carew there was Pat Leahy's Market and Max's Meat Market. Another fond memory is going to the end of Governor Street to watch the Our Lady of Hope Drum Corps march by.

Sue Vakakis recalls the days when the moth-ers in the neighborhood brought their kids to the Van Horn wading pool. The mothers would visit while the kids played in the pool.

Other fond memories of the neighborhood are going to Highlands Drug Store, Wenger's Bakery with their wonderful jelly doughnuts and Schmer-horn's Fish Market on Armory Street with the long line outside of the store on meatless Fridays.

George Chartier lived on Armory and Gov-ernor Streets in the 1960s and had a paper route that covered Grover, Cleveland and Sullivan Streets. George wrote a tribute to Dr. Lewis Blackmer in an unpublished short story entitled, *The Last House Call.* Dr. Blackmer was one of four Hungry Hill doctors in residence on Hungry Hill who made house calls. Doctors Greaney, Conway, Haggerty and Blackmer lived in the neighborhood, had their offices in their homes and made house calls. Greaney, Conway and Haggerty were the front runners in earlier times. Dr. Blackmer picked up the thread and kept this brand of medicine going into the 1960s.

Those were the days of one-car families and at-home mothers who were grateful to have a local doctor come to the house and treat their children. George recalls Dr. Blackmer's back-breaking schedule—house calls in the morning, hospital visits in the early afternoon and office hours in the evening when the waiting room was always full. He describes Dr. Blackmer as looking and sounding like the actor Broderick Crawford, a gruff manner, but a gentleness with young patients which included a supply of lollipops in his coat pocket.

Hamlet Street

Hamlet Street was known on city maps at one time as Carey's Farm or Carey's cow flop. The Patrick Carey family with their ten children, had a cow, a horse and several pigs. The Serra family next door had rabbits and chickens. This was officially a city neighborhood but the setting was very pastoral.

Ledyard Street

Dr. Francis Haggerty lived and worked out of his home on Ledyard Street for 40 plus years. He was a general practitioner who made house calls. His waiting room with its tall leather chairs was always full; some patients would be dozing while waiting their turn. He was small man with a vast knowledge of the human condition and, he wrote the book on bedside manner. He was always humming and made you feel better just by talking to him.

Laurence Street, et al

Living on Laurence Street and other streets in the "patch" area of Liberty Heights had its advantages whenever a plumber was needed. Jim Wynne lived on Nottingham Street and made many weekend calls when neighbors had plumbing emergencies. His son Bill now runs the family business.

One event that all the kids on Laurence Street looked forward to a few times a year was the softball game in the vacant lot next to the Morris house when many of the men on the street joined in with Smalley Beaulieu and George Bentley leading the teams.

Liberty Street

Murray Harris remembers the Tait Brothers Coal Company at the bottom of the hill on Liberty Street that sold several kinds of coal and coke. Anthracite coal was a hard coal that lasted a long time in the furnace, but it required a starter. Tait Brothers had a grinder to grind large chunks of anthracite into smaller pieces called pea coal, which could be used with a few sticks of wood to start the fire.

During the Depression, many families could not afford to buy a ton of coal so Tait Brothers had the pea coal available in 25- pound bags. They also sold 25- pound bags of coke. Harris Market, ran by Murray's family, realized the importance of these smaller sources of fuel so they stocked a large inventory of them. More than once, Murray's parents instructed him and his brother Seymour to deliver bags of coal at no charge to Mrs. Sullivan and others whom they feared were without heat. These small amounts of heating fuel were life savers during hard times.

Steve and David Tougias are the third generation of Tougias Baking Company located at the corner of Woodmont and Liberty Streets. The bakery was started in 1904 by their grandfather, Elias Tougias who immigrated from Greece in the 1890s.

Formerly known as the Athens Bakery which once featured pies and cakes as well as their signature crusty bread, the name was changed to Tougias and the family concentrated on bread and rolls only. To this day, Steve and David make bread the same way that their grandfather did using all natural ingredients, no chemicals or additives.

In the days when big Sunday dinners were the norm, the bakery was open on Sundays to accommodate the large number of people who stopped in after church to buy bread and rolls for dinner. Even now, they are mainly a wholesale business but they are open to retail orders and will accommodate anyone who calls in an order for bread or rolls.

Attached to the Tougias Baking Company at 881 Liberty is Casey's Barber Shop at the former location of the Liberty Register store. Tom Casey has operated this shop for 35 years. Tom lived at 104 Wilbur Street for 50 years and is known to many Hungry Hill people.

Through the years, he had a loyal clientele who liked to socialize and pass the time with other men from the neighborhood and, of course, get a trim from their favorite barber. At this writing, Tom was still open most weekdays.

Middle Street

For decades, Middle Street had long-term residents. The Viglianos, the Wilburs, the Wescotts, the Bowens, the Heffernons, the Brunos, the Frechettes, the Gallants, the Balardinis, the Gilmans and others lived in the area for many years and were good neighbors.

A notable long-term resident was Miceál O'Ceárna (Mike Carney), an Irish immigrant from the Blasket Islands who can best be described as a cultural ambassador. He and his wife, Maureen, and their four children, Maureen, Kathleen, Noreen and Michael enjoyed 37 years on Middle Street and took great pride in keeping up their home. Their house was located on the extension to Middle Street, which at one time, was part of the goat fields.

Miceál was one of the many Blasket Islanders who immigrated to this country and settled on Hungry Hill in Springfield when the Irish government forced the evacuation of the island. When he arrived in this country in 1948, three uncles and five aunts had preceded him. He was the first of five brothers and a sister to come to

America and he became a sponsor for some of them to immigrate. Eventually, he had more relatives living here than in Ireland. Prior to buying his house on Middle Street, he lived briefly on Sherbrooke, Mooreland and Armory Streets.

Miceál went to work for the A&P on Liberty Street where he worked hard, took business classes and became part of management. After his retirement he became a security officer at the Hall of Justice in Springfield.

Though Miceál was proud to be an American, he always remained close to his island roots. His efforts to promote Irish culture reached far and wide. He taught Gaelic language classes at the High School of Commerce, started a Gaelic Football Team in Springfield; served as President of the John Boyle O'Reilly Club for 10 years and took part in the mortgage negotiations for their new building on Progress Avenue. He was able to do that by taking time off from his job to attend a "wake." He served as Grand Marshall of the Springfield Division of the Holyoke St. Patrick's Day Parade. Miceál and his wife, Maureen were instrumental in establishing the Blasket Island Visitors Center in Dunquin and the Great Blasket Island National Historical Park.

Their legacy to the country of their birth is the initiation of the Blasket Island Bursary, which will award a scholarship each year to an Irish college student. The first year was exceptional as two scholarships were awarded. Miceál and Maureen, along with Padraig Firtear, Micheál de Mordha and Micheál and Lorcan O'Cinneide made this possible. Miceál was awarded an honorary doctorate in Celtic Literature by the National University of Ireland at Maynooth. He is listed in *"Who's Who Among Irish Americans"* and his photograph appears in *"To Love Two Countries"* a book about the Irish emigration to America. He is very humble about these honors and is truly amazed that a "fisherman's son from the island" could attain such recognition.

If Miceál has a personal mantra that he lives by, it would probably be *room for improvement.* His pursuits included self- improvement by education, spending time and effort to improve the life of the Irish community in Springfield, expanding and improving knowledge of Irish history by his work on the Blasket Visitors Center and improving the youth of Ireland by education through the Blasket scholarship program.

MillerStreet

A tribute to Van Horn Park

Jane Doherty O'Donoghue recalls growing up on Miller Street in a first-floor, five-room tenement. Her widowed mother raised six children alone in the depths of the Great Depression. The street was mostly tenement houses with large families that provided a huge choice of friends. A neighbor estimated that at one time, there were about 100 youths of all ages living there. Van Horn Park was their back yard where they spent countless creative hours during every season of the year.

Springtime brought pussy willows, new green leaves and lots of mud to play in. Baseball practice began again and kids sorted and counted marbles for some serious games.

Summertime meant swimming in the paddle pool, enjoying the playground, learning crafts and exploring the entire park. Swimming was not allowed in the two large ponds but they were great for pollywogging. Every July 4th, there was a fireworks display over the reservoir pond attended by the entire neighborhood.

In the *fall*, the park was alive with football games, practice sessions for high school teams and groups of people enjoying the fresh autumn air.

Winters meant sledding and skating. The ponds froze early and hundreds of people were skating at any given time. The ice house on the larger side of the pond always had a fire in the fireplace to keep warm when lacing skates. A popular priest, Father John Sexton, used to form a "whip" and have a long line of kids speeding across the pond.

In addition to Van Horn Park, Miller Street had many other benefits. It had a small store attached to a house where items such as bread, canned goods and penny candy were sold. It was walking distance to the Liberty branch library, the Liberty Theater and Our Lady of Hope Church and there were three bus lines close by.

Another plus was having wonderful neighbors who were protective of Jane's widowed mother. One time when tricksters cut the Doherty clotheslines, Jimmy and Mike Houlihan took lines from their aunt, Mrs. Lynch, and replaced the cut lines. Their reasoning was that their uncle was working and could afford it better than Mrs. Doherty.

During one long cold winter, the kids on the street were delighted when another neighbor, Mr. Conway, built a snow sculpture shaped like an elephant in the empty lot. This iced over and became an ideal fun place to climb and slide all winter!

Miller was a street where religious vocations were prevalent. In the late 40s and early

50s, four Miller Street girls of Irish American descent, Catherine Doherty, Margaret (Peggy) Nihill, Mary O'Connor and Mary (Mae) Barrett joined the Sisters of Saint Joseph. They all persevered in their calling and served their community in various ways.

Newbury Street

Eleanor Powell, the dancer and movie star, lived on Newbury Street and attended Liberty School. Murray Harris recalls that she took dance lessons with his sister in downtown Springfield.

Tommy Shea, noted columnist for *The Republican,* grew up on Newbury Street and recalls as a young boy being in Fulton's Market with his mother when one of the customers in the store looked at him and said, "well, you've got the map of Ireland on your face!" Tommy was shocked and ran home to look in a mirror to see if he could see a map on his face.

Tommy is a longtime fan and friend of renowned singer and songwriter Willie Nile, who has performed with Bruce Springsteen, the Ramones and Ringo Starr. At one of his local appearances in 2011, Willie performed a song called *There's a Diamond Shining on Hungry Hill* that he wrote as a tribute to Tom's father, John "The Diamond" Shea.

Sue Moore-Drumm recalls when her family ran the popular Cal's Variety on Newbury Street. Her great-grandmother started the business as a grocery store called The Unique Market and her grandfather Loyal K. Moore delivered groceries in a wagon, which led to founding his own trucking company, Moore's Delivery.

Sue had an idyllic childhood on Hungry Hill surrounded by grandparents, aunts, uncles and cousins all living together on the same block and playing together on Tacoma and David Streets.

For about five years, Sue ran the store, which was alive with memories of her grandparents' time including the wooden wagon used to deliver groceries. She closed the store to raise her own family and the building is now rented out and operates as a day spa.

Nottingham Street, et al

Sister Kathleen Keating, retired president of Elms College, remembers her childhood on Nottingham Street in the 1930s and 1940s as being part of a neighborhood of different faiths and ethnic backgrounds; people trying to survive and supporting one another, often with exceptional generosity. Some of her best memories are of long summer evenings when the neighborhood kids would gather to play tag or hide-and-goseek and then sit on the porch to listen to ghost stories. She describes her early years on Hungry Hill as "the world's best start" which gave her a wonderful foundation in life which she was able to build upon.

For decades, Nottingham Street was a magnet for patriots beginning with the immigrants who brought a rich history with them. Tom Welch of Nottingham Street came over in 1922 after serving in the Kerry No. 1 Brigade of Michael Collins' fledgling IRA volunteers led by Dingle commander Sean Moriarty. The Kerry Brigade had several other members from Springfield listed on its 1921-1922 roster: Lt. William Hurley, Lt. John J. Johnson, Quartermaster Pat Ashe, Sgt. Pat Coughlin, John McKenna, Pat Linehan, Tim Linehan, Maurice O'Connor and Alec Kevane. Tom was a quiet man and a true patriot who had zero tolerance for "bar room patriots." In 1972, he was invited back to Ireland to celebrate the 50th anniversary of his regiment. His son Bob Welch brought both parents to Ireland for this celebration.

Fred "Tripoli" Alovis of Nottingham Street, got his nickname from his service in the Italian Army in Tripoli and later served in the U.S. army during World War I. His property was one of the more interesting ones in the area. His son

Robert "Meatball" Alovis once placed a claw-foot bathtub on its side in the front yard with ALOVIS painted on it, which is still there. Fred had a car repair business in his yard among a gaggle of geese that were vicious and chased anyone who entered the yard. They also stopped traffic on Nottingham Street by going after moving cars including police cruisers. Fred was one of the founders of the Marconi Club and had his own bocce court in the back of his house. He made Italian wine once a year which he shared with neighbors. Every Christmas, Fred had a Christmas tree business which he operated from his yard. Nottingham Street neighbors have fond memories of this colorful, good man.

John J. Fitzgerald or "Jack Fitz" of 333 Nottingham Street brought a burning patriotic spirit with him to this country. As a young man in Ireland, he was an active participant in the struggle for Irish independence from England. During the Easter Uprising, Jack was part of the Irish volunteers in County Kerry, later called the IRA. During the Black and Tan War or War of Independence, he fought with the Kerry Brigade under the leadership of Austin Stack. They fought for a 32-county republic and would not accept partition by England. When treaty negotiations in London, led by Michael Collins, ended in defeat for the anti-treaty side and six counties remained under

British rule, Jack knew there was no future in Ireland for Republicans and probable imprisonment if they stayed. So, in 1923, he and a good friend, Jack Ashe, left Ireland under assumed names and went by boat to Canada where he lived and worked for a year before coming to America and settling in Springfield. When the Irish Free State granted amnesty for former civil war Republicans, he returned to Ireland to obtain his legal documents necessary for citizenship and also to marry Deborah Fitzgerald of Melbourne Street.

Jack kept his patriotic spirit alive by membership in Clan Na Gael in Springfield, which held yearly commemorations of the Easter Uprising. This always included a reading of the same proclamation that was read in front of the General Post Office in Dublin in 1916. Jack lived his life as a man of principle, devoted to his family and deeply committed to his religious faith. Above all, he was proud to be an American and could name all of the presidents in order.

Another Irish immigrant and friend, Mike Kane, lived one street over on Parallel Street. Mike was a "boy scout" during the conflict in Ireland. These were young boys who carried messages and warnings of British patrol activities.

In addition to their patriotic leanings, both Jack Fitz and Mike also brought music with them when they emigrated. "Jack Fitzgerald's Irish Minstrels" was a well-known musical group, which was an integral part of the Irish community's social and cultural life. Bo Fitz recalls that in good weather, when the windows were open, you could hear both his father and Mike in their respective homes, practicing on their accordions.

Jack's three children, Kevin, Joan and Robert Emmett, carried on the Irish Republican ideals and the Irish music tradition that they grew up with on Nottingham Street. Kevin and Robert Emmett (Bo) were Irish singers who performed locally. Bo was part of the original Dustmen group and currently he performs with the Yank-Celt Band.

Nottingham Street and vicinity had many losses during World War II. Among them were William Sullivan, who lost his life in the Battle of the Bulge and Edmund Wynne, who was a POW in the Pacific. Also, the Cormier family of Littleton Street lost two sons and John Cabey of Laurence Street died in France.

The next generation on Nottingham Street and its surrounding area continued to produce military men. Tom Welch's son Thomas (Gomo) served in the military as did three sons in the Speliopoulos family. Jackie and Jimmy Meara, Tom and Joe Martin, Joe and Charlie Mitchell,

Al and Andy Dedeurwaerder, Jack and Harry Frasier, Jim Murphy, Tom Sullivan, Jack Evans, Paul and Bernie Sexton and "Chubby" Kelleher, a career man in the Navy, were all from Nottingham Street. Also, surrounding Nottingham Street, Nick Lolas of Griffin Street served in the U.S. Navy; Laurence Street had Andrew "Bud" Cabey who served in the Army; Bill Cabey, U.S. Marine Corps; and Charles Svennson, a Navy man who was stationed at Pearl Harbor during the war and eventually moved back to Hawaii. A generation later, Dick Morris entered the U.S. Coast Guard and made it a career. Timmy Cabey and his brother Buddy served in Vietnam, Timmy in the Marines and Buddy in the Army, Paul Fennyery of Griffin Street served in the Army and Mike Morris opted for the Army Reserves.

A well-known local resident, Charles "Tuna" Sumares grew up on Nottingham Street in the 1960s. His love of classic cars developed into an annual car show *"Tuned by Tuna"* held at the Smith & Wesson grounds. This worthwhile event draws hundreds of people each year and the proceeds go to Shriners' Hospital.

Phoenix Street

Jim "Red" Garvey tells of growing up on the hill in the 1930's when one of his best friends was Kevin "Mike" Carey of Hamlet Street. Mrs. Carey always encouraged Mike, Jim and several of their friends to spend evenings at the Carey's house, rather than on the streets. They would have a great time dancing and there was always food–milk (right from the cow) and wonderful pies that Mrs. Carey made for them.

Jim also talks about the Liberty Theater and their hazardous way of getting in to see a movie without paying. Jim and three or four of his friends would pool their money, which meant checking the ground at Bottle Park for change and panhandling, for a few cents to get enough to pay for one admission to the Liberty, which was then ten cents. One of their crew would pay to get in and would sit in the front row near the stage. When the usher Charlie Healey wasn't looking, the one who paid to get in would crawl under the stage to the coal bin area where there was a window and open the window to let the other kids in. Then they would all crawl through the coal bin and under the stage and wait until the coast was clear and one at a time, would find a seat in various parts of the theater. They were always afraid that the usher would notice the streaks of coal dust on them and fig- ure out their game. They took turns confessing this scenario to Father Sexton at Our Lady of Hope Church.

Retired firefighter Jim Harrigan talks about growing up on Phoenix Street in the 1950s when the sounds from the neighborhood included the radio blasting the rosary from Mr. Garvey's house. Jim tells of his grandmother, Margaret Boland Harrigan who was the second woman in Springfield to have a driver's license, the police chief's wife being the first. One of Jim's fondest memories from Hungry Hill was meeting Hopalong Cassidy. William Boyd, the movie and TV actor made an appearance on Kendall Street at a store that distributed his sponsor's national brand of bread. Jim was about seven years old and showed up with his sixguns and cowboy hat to meet his hero.

Phoenix Terrace

Phoenix Terrace had some memorable residents. One was Flora "Flo" Millette, who was a woman ahead of her time in the public service sector. Flo graduated from Elms College and earned a master's degree from Springfield College, where she was a member of the faculty. Her major work was with girls and young women in conflict with the law. She was a police officer, then a probation officer and finally, Assistant Chief Probation Officer in Springfield District Court.

Her achievements in the court system included co-authoring a manual of guidelines for juvenile probation and police officers in Massachusetts and membership in the Massachusetts Probation Association, Mass Council of Probation Officers for Juveniles; New England Regional Group of the National Council on Crime and Delinquency and advisory chairman of the Mercy Hospital School of Nursing. In addition, she taught CCD at Our Lady of Hope church and worked with many local civic, religious and education groups involved with children. In 1999 she received the Elms College Victoria Joseph Award for service to children.

Another well-known, immensely popular resident of Phoenix Terrace was Dante Christofori, who was a native son of Hungry Hill. After graduating from Trade High School where he was class president, he worked as a millwright for Perkins Machine & Gear and then became an ironworker at the Seabrook Nuclear Plant for many years. He served in the Navy and was a founding member of American Legion Post 430. His wife, Florence, was a charter member of their Ladies Auxiliary. He and Florence had five children, Carol, William, Judi, Lori and Joe.

One of the first signs of spring on Phoenix Terrace was Dante riding his bike up and down the streets, visiting friends or heading to a ball-game. He loved Van Horn youth sports and many a Van Horn ballplayer can remember him in the stands yelling advice as only he could do.

Virginia Alovis Nascimento who lived on Nottingham Street recalls that their dog would wait by the fence for Dante to walk by on his way home from the Marconi Club. The dog knew that Dante always had a treat for him.

Dante loved his role as the "Italian son" of Hungry Hill. He knew more Irish songs than most of his Irish friends and went to Ireland six times with the O'Brien's Corner trips. In addition, he was "Mr. Fixit" to his family and friends who could go to him when they needed expertise in repairing a leaky pipe, a door that was stuck, an electrical problem, an oil burner that wouldn't work on a cold winter's night or just someone to listen to their problems. He had the knack of making people feel better about their surroundings and about themselves, a rare trait then and now.

In the 1970s, Phoenix Terrace was the site of several Hungry Hill Block Parties organized by the Hungry Hill Civic Association. The street was blocked off at Freeman Terrace and a stage was set up for Irish musicians to perform.

The James and Mary Fitzgerald home on Phoenix Terrace was the "home of the Dustmen," the Irish singing group that featured Bo Fitzgerald, Bruce Fitzgerald, Jeff Sullivan, Tom Grassetti and John Tabb. Bo Fitzgerald credits his Uncle Jim, who had a beautiful singing voice, for being an inspiration for this group as well as his father's musical group, Jack Fitzgerald's Irish Minstrels.

Sherbrooke Street

Some Hungry Hill residents were legends in their own time. Bill Hogan of Sherbrooke Street was part of a large family of motorcycle enthusiasts. Bill was the "Fonz" of the HH/East Springfield area. His claim to fame was that he once rode his motorcycle through the halls of Trade High School, (now Putnam Vocational). Others talk about him riding his bike down the steep front steps of Van Sickle.

Strong Street

Lorraine Artioli Serra remembers living at the end of Strong Street when Paul Hogan's horses would get loose from Liberty Street and gallop down their street. She also remembers living on the corner of Border and Carew Streets where her father would let the Sherwood's goats graze on their extra lot.

Wolcott Street

Linda Nickett of 23 Wolcott Street won the *Miss Springfield* pageant in the early 1960s. Her house was one of many on that end of the street taken by eminent domain for the highway in 1967.

The Shea sisters, Ann and Mary, have lived on Wolcott Street since they immigrated to this country from Dingle, County Kerry, Ireland. They raised their families here and were active participants in the Irish community which led to their receiving an award from the 2012 St. Patrick's Day Parade Committee.

Van Horn Park

Joan McCarthy Ryan lived on several Hungry Hill Streets; Armory, Home, Miller and Van Horn Place before her final move to a house located in Van Horn Park. Joan was Springfield's "first lady" for ten years. She married Charlie Ryan who served as Mayor for five terms, three in the 1960s and two from 2004-2007. Her brother, Donnie McCarthy, was a well-known Irish musician who played at many weddings, including the author's wedding, as well as numerous other gatherings.

Hungry Hill Nicknames

By Dan Keyes

Not unlike other ethnic neighborhoods throughout the United States, Hungry Hill had a plethora of nicknames, some of them physically descriptive, some pejorative and many of unknown provenance. Herewith is a list of names that I can recall. In cases where the name is derogatory or belittling, the last name is omitted.

Ginger Cunningham	Villa Boland
Brud Cullinan	Congo Keyes
Banjo Cullinan	Mope_____
Putty Nose Sullivan	Butch Biglin
Mustard Kennedy	Dapper Hayes
Bunny O'Malley	Soss Maloney
Sis Leary	Wallop Moynahan
Sharkey Dineen	Righty Keough
Biddy Doyle	Pie McNulty
Peanuts Ryan	Jazz Gordon
Rabbit (Rab) Murphy	Gin bottles ....
Porky Powers	Gus Doyle

Whale sh**	Hiney Batt
Wimpy ……	Bud Mallaney
JellyDonuts Foley	Cowboy Kelleher
Wicky Sears	Green Tees Flannery
Gop O'Brien	Snuffy Smith
Skibereen Donovan	Geezer_____
Eggsy Coughlin	Bull Fabbri
Monk Bowler	Lefty Keough
Serge Foley	Heavy Legs Garvey
Squaw Keyes	Chinky Coughlin
Trapper Garvey	Skinny Grover
Sesty Burke	Bobo Griffin
Skunk Sullivan	Unk O'Connor
Donkey Herlihey	Peewee Moore
Zum Berard	Goat Regan
Sailor Burke	Buck Donoghue
Buster Griffin	Tinky Rowe
Baldy Kennedy	Scotty Brown
Pickles Harrington	Farmer Rice

Ace O'Connell	Shrimp McDonald
Buckets Demetrion	Dutch Metzger
Tug Boat Sullivan	Crow Allen
Ferry Boat Sullivan	Scooter Woods
Youngla Herlihey	Beans Curran
Smiles Gilmore	Batty Shea
Hock Allen	Sh**head_____
Bunty Hoar	Wiggy Biglin
Happy Houlihan	Clinkers _____
Speed Misit	Tossy Shea
Rags Misit	Spot McDonald
Toby Fenton	Midge Reilly
Pop McNamara	Boots Vecchiarelli
Babe Manfredi	Bundy Burns
Rod Kane	The Gomeral (Gomel)
FuzzTop Coughlin	"The Boy Cop" O'Connell
Pic O'Neil	Ki Yi Stahovich
Bibbers Dalton	Shadow Lynch
Tip Appleby	Husky Sullivan

Morg Foley   Suitcase Simpson

Duddy Moylan   Goober Woods

Jada Woods   Spud Murphy

Bones Martin   Dee Dee_____

Goof _____

ADDITIONAL NICKNAMES

(Source: A Hungry Hill Trinity)

Beppo Devine	Skipper James
Willum Garvey	Junkie O'Connell
Wimp Sullivan	
Ace Manning	Fritzy Crogan
Bluey Bessone	Fat Foley
Fuzzy Coughlin	Tip O'Neal
Lado Haggerty	Spot McDonnell
Muck McGovern	Rosco Russell
Cowboy Haggerty	Bunty Hoar
Wimpy Lynch	Moon Russell
Hawk Zisk	Pee Wee Moore
Archie Lynch	Gomo Russell
Kryl Bryda	Tank Murphy
Gomo Welch	Mel Roncalli
Beep Bryda	Moose Kennedy
Noo Noo Montesi	Kid Calloo
Huck Kane	Jaymo Murphy
Perry Pop	Red O'Shaunessey

Banjo Eyes Keough	Jughead Keough
Boogie Bentley	Mickey McMahon
Butch Biglin	Snots O'Connor
Blinky Carney	Clinkers Kennedy
Big Unk O'Connor	Honky Sawyer
'B' Maloney	Mustard Kennedy
Little Unk O'Connor	Yacko Dowd
Moose McCarthy	Snake Johnson
Scar Bowler	Flyshit Dowd
Ty Tyburski	BeBop Walsh
Pots Long	Red Garvey
Baldy Kennedy	Giggie Bryda
Gaf Gaffney	Fod O'Donnell
Mouse Manning	Jelly Donuts Foley
Ox McCarthy	Ripper Valenti

HUNGRY HILL TRIVIA QUIZ

Created by Bunty Hoar- courtesy
of Dan Keyes

1. Former name of Newbury and Nottingham Streets

2. Name the dump and also old reservoir located in woods beyond Pembroke Street

3. The number of the trolley on the Carew to East Spfld. line

4. Name the market on Carew Street, a block or two west of Raymond Place

5. Name the athletic field next to the Armory St. Fire Station

6. Name the pharmacy located at the corner of Liberty and Armory Streets

7. Two most remembered Acorns football coaches

8. Name of radio sportscaster from Melha Street

9. Owner of market at Liberty and Grover Streets

10. First school committeeman from Ward 2

11. All Western Mass. halfback from Classical High School 1939

12. Chain store located on Carew Street, near Newbury

13. Cattle dealer who lived on Wait Street

14. The year Tommy O'Connor went to the Legislature

15. He lost Registry of Deeds race to Eddie Boland

16. Jewish hardware store owner from Parkside Street

17. Former Acorn football player who served on the Springfield License Commission

18. The two best basketball referees from Hungry Hill – late 1930's

19. He defeated Gene Sweeney for state representative

20. He succeeded Eddie Boland as state representative

21. When did Shriner's Hospital open?

22. What was the name of the movie theater on Cleveland Street and who ran it?

23. Name the variety store at corner of Liberty & Kendall streets

24. Name of market located at corner of Armory and Cleveland Streets

25. Name of former hardware store located near Wenger's Bakery

ANSWERS TO HUNGRY HILL TRIVIA

1. Chicopee Road was Nottingham Street to Carew and picked up again on Newbury Street

2. Hallwrights (Horize)

3. Number 20

4. Kantor's Market

5. Engine #9 Bowl

6. Kazin's

7. Dapper Hayes and Sharkey Dineen

8. Bob Feldman

9. Mr. Harris

10. Charlie Haggerty

11. Howie Welch

12. A.H. Phillips store

13. Max Girant

14. 1951

15. C. Wesley Hale

16. Mr. Alpert

17. Bill Marasi

18. Jim Conners and Gus Winters

19. John Curley

20. Gene Sweeney

21. 1925

22. Cleveland Theater – Mr. Kelleher

23. Rice and Murphy

24. Magni's

25. Ring's

® *Joseph D Christofori*

Thanks for the memories......

® *Joseph D Christofori*

Courtesy – Joseph D. Christofori

Courtesy – Joseph D Christofori

The Liberty Theatre as it appeared in the '30s.